New Perspectives on
Jazz

Report on a National Conference Held at Wingspread

Racine, Wisconsin

September 8–10, 1986

Sponsored by
National Jazz Service Organization

and
Berklee College of Music
University of Massachusetts–Amherst
The Keland Endowment Fund of the Johnson Foundation
in cooperation with
Indiana University School of Music
and the
National Endowment for the Arts

New Perspectives on Jazz

David N. Baker, *Editor*

Smithsonian Institution Press
Washington and London

Editor: Duke Johns
Designer: Janice Wheeler

Library of Congress Cataloging-in-Publication Data
New perspectives on jazz : report on a national conference held at
Wingspread, Racine, Wisconsin, September 8–10, 1986 / David N. Baker,
editor; sponsored by National Jazz Service Organization . . . [et al.].
p.   cm.
ISBN 0-87474-332-X (alk. paper).--
ISBN 0-87474-985-9 (pbk.: alk. paper)
1. Jazz music--Congresses.   I. Baker, David N., 1931–   .
II. National Jazz Service Organization.
ML3505.9.N48   1990
781.65--dc20   89-11264

British Library Cataloguing-in-Publication Data is available

Manufactured in the United States of America

98 97 96 95 94 93 92 91   5 4 3 2

∞ The paper used in this publication meets the minimum requirements of
the American National Standard for Permanence of Paper for Printed
Library Materials Z39.48–1984.

Contents

Foreword

The National Jazz Service Organization (NJSO), formed to nurture the growth and enhancement of jazz as an American art form, includes all forms of jazz music in its definition of jazz and recognizes it as a gift to the world through the Afro-American experience. NJSO educates, informs, communicates, and networks to enhance the status of jazz.

New Perspectives on Jazz, a project of the NJSO Board of Directors designed by a planning committee and implemented by staff and consultants, illustrates NJSO's deep and continuing commitment to this philosophy. In September 1986, a cross section of leaders in American jazz met at Wingspread, the conference center of the Johnson Foundation in Racine, Wisconsin, for three days of intensive discussions.

The purpose of the conference was to reexamine the jazz field for those involved in it, explain it for those not familiar with it, and direct it for those responsible for its future. This mid-decade look at the jazz field provided direction for its development into the 21st century.

The conference focused on four commissioned papers and a prepared response to each paper. These commissioned papers and responses are now published in this anthology, *New Perspectives on Jazz*. Following the conference, two additional papers were requested—one from a leader in the music industry who participated in the conference, and one from a scholar who was not able to participate but was able to review the prepared papers and responses. These papers are included in this publication as examples of the thought and discussion that we hope will continue over the next decade.

"The American Jazz Music Audience," a report prepared for the National Jazz Service Organization by the director of research of the National Endowment for the Arts, was released at the Wingspread conference, and a summary is included in this publication. This comprehensive analysis is based on data derived from the 1982 Survey of Public Participation in the Arts, which was sponsored by the National Endowment for the Arts and conducted by the U.S. Census Bureau. For the first time in recent history, questions concerning the jazz audience can be answered with factual information.

New Perspectives on Jazz represents the most comprehensive exploration of jazz in this nation by some of the most recognized authorities on the subject. This is the first effort to deal with issues related to jazz that are not limited to forms, styles, and personalities of jazz, moving beyond sociological concerns to address cultural, historical, and economic issues related to the survival of an art form that is uniquely American, rooted in the Afro-American experience. This publication joins NJSO's list of original documents designed to increase the body of knowledge about and for the jazz field.

Thanks are due to Henrietta Sanford, director of programs at NJSO, who coordinated the meeting at Wingspread, and to consultant Victoria Sharpley for her role during and following the conference, which included preparing two public affairs radio broadcasts as part of the

Johnson Foundation's series, "Conversations from Wingspread," and coordinating the manuscripts for publication.

Appreciation is expressed to the Keland Endowment Fund of the Johnson Foundation and to the National Endowment for the Arts for their continued support; to the cosponsoring institutions, the Berklee College of Music, the University of Massachusetts–Amherst, and the Indiana University School of Music; to members of the planning committee; to conference participants; and to the presenters and respondents.

Special appreciation is expressed to the Smithsonian Institution and the Smithsonian Institution Press for making this publication possible.

Eunice Lockhart-Moss
Executive Director
National Jazz Service Organization
1985–88

Opening Statement

This is an exciting conference with possibilities and parallels. The Statement of Purpose leaves everything open to us to make it productive and enjoyable. To make the meeting important for the artists in jazz and the people in this country and around the world who support this great creative spirit, we have been encouraged to concentrate on four areas of consideration: the influence of jazz on concert music; the evolution of jazz; jazz criticism; and the economics of jazz. These are four very broad areas, but we can be guided by the papers and responses prepared for each area. These papers, responses, and discussions by this group will serve as the basis for further discussion, reflection, and understanding of jazz.

John Conyers, Jr.
Congressman, State of Michigan, First District
United States House of Representatives

Opening Statement

I bring you greetings from the board of trustees, President Lee Elliott Berk, students, faculty, and staff of the Berklee College of Music, a college whose history is intimately tied to the history and development of jazz. It gives us great pleasure to serve as a cosponsor in the investigation of "New Perspectives on Jazz," America's only indigenous music form. This symposium will, we hope, be helpful in significantly increasing the overall visibility, acceptance, and appreciation of our art form.

Warrick L. Carter
Dean of the Faculty
Berklee College of Music

Opening Statement

On behalf of Chancellor Joseph Duffey, I am delighted to bring you his greetings from the Amherst campus of the University of Massachusetts. Chancellor Duffey's commitment to public service, education, and the arts has been reflected in the positions he has held, including assistant secretary of state, U.S. Department of State, Bureau of Educational and Cultural Affairs; chairman of the National Endowment for the Humanities; fellowships and residencies at Harvard and Yale universities; and as a Rockefeller doctoral scholar.

It is appropriate to share a statement Chancellor Duffey often makes when speaking publicly about the arts: "In the world of the arts, jazz is America's distinct and unique art form."

Frederick C. Tillis
Director, Fine Arts Center; Associate Provost and Professor of Music
University of Massachusetts–Amherst

Opening Statement

I must begin by tipping my hat to John Conyers for coming and chairing an arts conference. It's the only time it has occurred since I've been chairman at the Endowment, and we are grateful to him.

I am privileged and honored to be here, and I can't think of anything that is more important than to be a part of the first major meeting of the National Jazz Service Organization, examining the problems and opportunities of what has already been described as that particularly American art form. There's nothing more important on my agenda.

I should also tip my hat in thanks to William Boyd, the president of the Johnson Foundation, for making these Wingspread facilities available for the meeting. It is a great pleasure for me to join you here.

It seems to me that the participation here at Wingspread of so many authorities on jazz, representatives of the music industry, the media, foundations and corporations, higher education, jazz organizations, and distinguished jazz artists promises to make this a landmark event in developing ideas on the future of jazz. As most of you know, the National Endowment for the Arts has been committed, since its early years, to furthering the growth and development of jazz. I would like to recount some of that history. Most of it happened before I became chairman, so I take no credit for it, but I think it underscores the Endowment's involvement over the years.

One of the first members of the National Council on the Arts was Ralph Ellison—the distinguished novelist, cultural critic, and jazz publicist—who was selected in 1985 by President Reagan to receive the National Medal of Arts. Ellison was the first National Council member to urge Endowment support of jazz, and in subsequent years his voice was echoed on the Council by two of the greatest figures in jazz, Duke Ellington and Billy Taylor. Billy Taylor is here with us today, as is Gunther Schuller, a former member of the National Council on the Arts, and others.

In 1968 the first Endowment jazz panel was formed. In 1969 a jazz grant was made to composer, arranger, and educator George Russell. The following year, the panel recommended seventeen grants to individuals and eleven grants to organizations: a total of about $20,000. Nancy Hanks commented that "Few projects in the history of the Endowment have been as rewarding and successful as our modest venture into the field of jazz."

The number of jazz grants reached 155 by 1975, amounting to a little over a half million dollars to ninety-three individuals and sixty-two organizations. Today, in 1986, our support represents 175 grants totaling $1,234,000. At least ten of the organizations represented here are, or have been, Endowment grantees, and ten conference participants have been jazz panelists. We thank you for that, for these panels are the heart of our system, and we could not make good judgments if some of you weren't willing to take some of your time and come to Washington to help us.

We initiated a jazz oral history project in 1977, and technical assistance grants and on-site evaluations were begun in 1981. The Jazz Masters awards program was initiated in 1982. Within the Endowment's Music Program, jazz is currently funded in the following grant categories: Jazz Fellowships for composition, performance, study, and special projects; Jazz Presenting Organizations for programs, management assistance, and special projects; and Jazz Ensembles.

Moreover, the Endowment's support for jazz is not confined to these specific categories. The Multi-Music Presenters, Festivals, and Recording categories include additional support for jazz. It is noteworthy that many symphony orchestras receiving support from the Endowment are now featuring an increasing number of jazz artists on their programs. Outside the Music Program, significant support for jazz is furnished by the Expansion Arts, Media Arts, Inter-Arts, and Folk Arts programs. Folk Arts, for example, helps to preserve the blues tradition that is at the root of jazz.

The Arts Endowment thus continues to share the basic objectives of everybody in this room—to increase professional opportunities for jazz artists and enhance all aspects of the jazz field as a vital and crucial dimension of American culture. As you know, this is the second Wingspread conference on jazz. In April 1984, the Arts Endowment and the Keland Endowment Fund cosponsored the planning meeting here at Wingspread that led to the creation of the National Jazz Service Organization. In August of that year, the National Council considered two grants in the amount of $50,000 each for initial operating expenses and for an executive director and support staff. We made those grants, notwithstanding our general rule that service organizations should acquire a track record before receiving Endowment funding, and that service organization funding should be reserved for specific projects and not general operating support. We did this because of our belief in the need for a national service organization to represent and help the field of jazz. In April 1985, NJSO was launched under the able direction of Eunice J. Lockhart-Moss.

You have before you the Endowment's principal contribution to this conference, a study entitled "The American Jazz Music Audience" by Harold Horowitz, the director of the Endowment's

Research Division. Harold has been referred to as "the Renaissance man" because he researches everything at the Endowment. You can be sure that whatever facts he presents to you are real facts, because he has gone over them with a fine-tooth comb, analyzing the statistical difficulties and working them out. He does not provide anything unless he has done it well.

As David Baker says in his introduction, this study "represents another step in the continuing partnership between the Endowment and the National Jazz Service Organization . . . a new framework and perspective for identifying and assessing ways to share the future of jazz." It is, therefore, a highly appropriate focus for this conference.

Harold's presentation, which is based upon data from the Endowment's Survey on Public Participation in the Arts, merits detailed consideration. It will promote discussion and surface questions some of you may not have thought about before. Without going into the findings, there is one thing the study shows that I would like to underscore. That is, there are enormous audiences for jazz and they take all forms. Audiences and support for jazz are increasing. It is a good time for jazz and for the National Jazz Service Organization to get in and help build this momentum even further, to bring jazz back to the forefront of America as it existed for decades in the 1920s, 30s, 40s, and 50s. That is, I would suggest, what your task is, in part, here.

We are glad to be helping to support this conference. What we hope will come out of it is a series of concrete suggestions as to where we can have the most effect in helping the art form of jazz and, most important, helping the art of jazz to reach Americans wherever they are. We're in the business to help, and we hope you will give us guidance.

Frank Hodsoll
Chairman
National Endowment for the Arts

Opening Statement

As Chairman Hodsoll has pointed out, this occasion seems like déjà vu for a lot of us. It seems only yesterday that we were here—sometimes paranoid, suspicious, and at times openly hostile to each other, because we were not convinced that this was not going to be another exercise in futility. I think that once we were convinced, it was difficult for us to imagine why anyone was not convinced of what we were about and what we were trying to do.

Wingspread was the birthplace of the National Jazz Service Organization, and we are back again with two of our original sponsors, the Keland Endowment Fund of the Johnson Foundation and the National Endowment for the Arts, at yet another milestone in the life of NJSO. We very much appreciate that these sponsors have tracked with us over these two crucial years. We are also most happy to have added other sponsors, including Berklee College of Music in Boston;

the University of Massachusetts–Amherst; and the Indiana University School of Music.

This conference plays an important part for us at NJSO in our planning and programming as we move closer to the National Center for Jazz in the nation's capital and toward the 21st century. The conference also gives us the opportunity to tell you how important you and your organizations are to us. You are our front line of communication—our collaborators, consultants, constituents, and colleagues. We need your ideas and input to our plans and development. The truth of the adage "when you want something done, ask a busy person" is borne out by your participation and your willingness to commit time, effort, and money in support of the objectives of this conference. Among those whose organizational skills and vision have contributed heavily to make this conference possible is the staff of NJSO and its consultants.

The purpose of this conference is to reexamine the jazz field for those involved in it, explain it for those not familiar with it, and direct it for those responsible for its future. The presenters and respondents are among the most respected, brilliant, and original thinkers in the field. They will be responsible for the initiation of the serious discussion of ideas and strategies essential for the enhancement and survival of jazz into the 21st century. We congratulate and thank our presenters and respondents for having the courage and integrity to accept our challenge to expose their innermost thoughts to scrutiny, criticism, and comment. We hope that these next few days will be fruitful and provocative, and that what transpires here will help us to better serve the music we love so deeply.

David N. Baker
President, National Jazz Service Organization
Distinguished Professor of Music and Chairman
Jazz Studies Department
Indiana University School of Music

New Perspectives on
Jazz

Harold Horowitz, *Presenter*

The American Jazz Audience

American jazz has been studied from many perspectives. The musical form itself, its origins and evolution, and the artists who perform it have become subjects for a large body of scholarly and critical literature. The audience for jazz, however, has not attracted the same kind of intensive study, and little information can be found in the open literature. Of course, the major recording companies conduct surveys of potential record buyers and of recorded music sales, and local radio stations have their surveys of listeners, but the results of such sales development research have not become widely available as an open literature. In the absence of reliable audience information, anecdotes and personal observations have been used. Differing viewpoints have been debated on such questions as the size and makeup of the audience for jazz. But until recently, there has not been an acceptable data source that might help to resolve some of the broad and widespread differences of opinion.

A significant step toward improving the understanding of the American jazz audience was taken when the National Endowment for the Arts commissioned the U.S. Bureau of the Census to collect information on the participation of adult Americans in a wide range of arts and cultural activities, including jazz. Development work for a Survey of Public Participation in the Arts started in 1979, and the first of two national surveys was fielded in 1982. A report containing a detailed statistical analysis of these data was first distributed at the "New Perspectives on Jazz" conference.* The following highlights from that report take the form of questions that are frequently asked, and the answers suggested by the data.

The statistical quality of this survey was high, and the probability sample of American adults that was drawn by the Bureau of the Census is large by usual standards. So it is possible to break down the information and reorganize it into many different combinations. The analysis shows that the American jazz audience is fairly complex and cannot be described simply in a few words without blurring many of its important features. There are many patterns within this audience, which includes people from diverse categories of residence, age, sex, race, education, and household income.

A one-line answer might be that the jazz audience is quite large, and mostly urban, young, white, well-educated, and from high income-level households. This simple answer may be technically correct as a description of the characteristics of the "typical" jazz audience, but it fails to explain the diversity in the patterns that showed up in the survey results. The readers of the following questions and answers should also be aware that survey results of samples of the population may vary somewhat from the results that would have been found if the entire population had been surveyed.

The question most often asked is, How large is the jazz audience? The answer is, quite large. When four kinds of participation are

---

*Harold Horowitz, "The American Jazz Music Audience," National Jazz Service Organization, Washington, D.C., 1986. This report is also available through libraries and information services with access to the Education Research Information System (ERIC). The ERIC document number is 280757.

combined, the jazz audience in 1982 included about 54 million individuals, or nearly one-third of all American adults. The four types of jazz participation measured in the survey were: attending live performances, listening to recordings, listening to the radio, and watching television. Obviously, there can be big differences in the quality or in the seriousness of the participation in these four different activities. Attending a live performance is considerably more demanding, in requiring the effort to go out and give undivided attention to a performance, than is listening to music on your auto radio for background while driving to work.

But we shouldn't be too quick to make such simple distinctions. The survey data indicate that, in general, older Americans tend toward the types of participation that are less physically demanding than attending live performances, such as listening to radio and watching television. The survey data also show a clear difference in the age distribution patterns of persons who attend live jazz performances and those who participate by means of the electronic media.

There is also a sobering information item found in the answers to questions about the kinds of music the public likes. Only about 43 million respondents answered that they liked jazz, which suggests that some of the "yes" responses to the participation questions were given by persons who do not actually like jazz, but may have caught some of it on a radio or television broadcast, perhaps inadvertently, or perhaps went along and did something that friends wanted to do while in a group or on a date. But even if we take the 43 million as our gross estimate rather than 54 million, the general conclusion remains the same: the jazz audience is quite large.

Question: How do the four different kinds of participation compare for their shares of the jazz audience? **Answer:** The largest jazz audience is for listening to recordings. Twenty percent of American adults (32 million) said they listened to jazz recordings at least once in the year preceding their survey interview. Following in size are the audiences for radio and for television, which are about 18 percent each (29 million each). The audience for live performances is the smallest, with 10 percent of adults (16 million). There is quite a bit of overlap in these four audiences, as is apparent by adding together the figures and comparing the sum to the gross audience size described in the preceding answer. When one examines the size of the audiences who participate in only one way, the television-only audience is the largest, with 5 percent of adults (8 million); the recording-listening-only audience second, with 3.5 percent (6 million); the radio-only audience next, with about 3 percent of adults (5 million); and the live-performance-only audience the smallest, with about 2 percent of adults (3 million). The highly dedicated jazz audience, which is the audience that participates in all four ways, has about 3 percent of adults (5 million).

Question: What does the survey show about the demographic characteristics of the jazz audience? **Answer:** The audiences for the four forms of participation display individual demographic patterns. There are certain similarities but there are also differences, so a complete description requires study of the statistical tables. Moreover, it is easy to become confused by the differences between the audience proportions of the publics in each subgroup or stratum (which are described in terms of concentrations or rates of participation), and the differences in terms of absolute numbers of persons in each subgroup or stratum. For example, as mentioned earlier, a simple answer regarding the racial makeup of the jazz audience is that it is mostly white. This answer obscures the black population's much higher rates of participation. Table 1 shows more clearly than words by themselves that blacks, when considered in proportion to their numbers, are much more frequent participants in each of the four audiences than whites. It is only when one takes the participation average for the entire population that the greater number of white persons becomes dominant.

Of all the demographic characteristics that were considered in the survey, the level of educational attainment emerges as the most important predictor of jazz participation. When the population is stratified by levels of educational attainment, the corresponding rates of participation in each of the four audiences were found to increase with education. The jazz recording audience illustrates the ranges that

Table 1
Rates of Jazz Participation by Race

Race	Number of Adults	Attend Live Events	Watch on TV	Listen on Radio	Listen to Recordings
Black	17,470,000	15%	28%	36%	36%
White	143,355,000	9%	17%	16%	18%
Other	3,750,000	9%	21%	23%	20%

were found in each of the four kinds of participation: only 5 percent of persons whose highest level of education was grade school said that they listened to jazz recordings, while 39 percent of the persons who had completed their first college degree and had also attended graduate school were listeners to jazz recordings. But educational attainment levels are not divided equally among the whole population, and most people have not attended graduate school. At the time of the survey, the highest educational attainment of nearly 40 percent of the adult population was graduation from high school, and another group of about 20 percent had completed some college but had not graduated. The majority of the jazz audiences come from these two large middle-education groups, even though the concentration or rates of participation are considerably greater for the smaller groups that have completed college and gone further with their educations.

Unlike educational attainment, the household income patterns for the four forms of participation are not consistent with each other. Jazz audience participation by means of attending live events and by listening to recordings follows patterns similar to those of educational attainment. For these, the concentration or rate of participation goes up with increasing household income, but the ranges are not as wide as for education. For the audience watching television, the differences are quite small as they ascend the income scale, and for respondents listening to the radio there are hardly any differences at all between the different income groups.

The characteristic of audience age generally shows a pattern of greater rates of participation by younger persons. This relationship is most striking for attenders of live performances, but the differences are much less for the other kinds of participation and, in the case of the audience watching television, the differences are quite small. Once again, one should pay attention to the numbers of persons in the various groups. In 1982, over 40 percent of the adult population was under 35 years of age, and the 35–44 age group included nearly 17 percent of the adult population. For these reasons, jazz audiences look fairly young, and the appeal of jazz to persons in the older age groups may be overlooked. Except for attendance at live performances, persons in the 45–74 age groups report substantial participation rates. Watching jazz performances on television and listening to jazz recordings are about as popular with persons in these older age groups as they are to persons in the younger age groups, and only slightly less so for listening to jazz on the radio.

When considered by the sex of the audience members, the patterns for the four kinds of participation are similar. The rates of participation by men are greater than for women in each of the four audiences, but the differences are small. On the other hand, there are more women in the adult population than there are men, so the numbers of persons of each sex work out to be nearly the same for each type of participation.

Question: Where do people go to hear live performances of jazz? **Answer:** The survey responses from people who only attend jazz performances differ quite a bit from the answers given by people who also attend other kinds of performing arts. The jazz-only attenders mentioned concert halls and auditoriums, nightclubs and coffeehouses, and parks and other open-air facilities as their most frequent places; each of these three categories was mentioned by at least 20 percent of the jazz-only attenders. The segment of the audience that attends other types of performing arts as well as jazz named two additional frequent performance places: college or university facilities, and theaters. Each of the five top performance places of the audience for multiple performing arts was cited by at least 30 percent of these attenders.

Question: Where does the jazz audience live? **Answer:** Again, a simple answer is not satisfying, because the distributions of the audiences for the four types of participation are not the same. The southern region has the largest number of attenders of live jazz performances, but the West, with the smallest population of the four regions, has the greatest rate of participation at live performances. Listeners to jazz recordings are found in about equal numbers in the four U.S. regions, while the number of live performance attenders varies substantially. The northeast region has the smallest number of attenders, but New York City has the largest jazz audience of any single city. The one generalization that can be made about the locations of jazz audiences is that they are extremely urban. For example, 13 percent of the persons who live in the central cities of metropolitan areas attend live performances, compared with 6 percent of the population living outside of metropolitan areas and with 4 percent of the people who live on rural farms.

Question: Do jazz audiences cross over into other performing arts? **Answer:** Correlation studies using the survey data show some crossover between the audience for jazz and the audiences for each of the other performing arts. For example, out of the audience for live performances of jazz, 9 percent also attend performances of opera, 14 percent also attend ballet performances, 31 percent also attend performances of plays, 34 percent also attend classical music and chamber music performances, and 41 percent also attend performances of musical plays.

Question: Is there a demand for increased attendance opportunities? **Answer:** About twice as many persons want to attend jazz performances compared to the number already attending them. The reasons most often given for not attending were: not enough time, cost, not available, and too far to go. The last two distance-related reasons were cited by 22 percent and 13 percent, respectively, of the respondents who wanted to increase their attendance. Most of the attenders at live performances were in the youngest age groups; the survey also found that about 60 percent of the persons who want to attend more jazz performances are in the 18–24 age group, which suggests a participation demand that may persist for a long time.

Gunther Schuller, *Presenter*

The Influence of Jazz on the History and Development of Concert Music

The relationship between jazz and classical "concert music" has always been both profound and fragile, and frequently confusing and misinterpreted. "Profound" because certain aspects of the European classical tradition, particularly its harmony and to some extent its melodic, rhythmic, and instrumental traditions, were from the outset fundamental and inextricable parts of the evolution of jazz as a distinct musical language. That is, of course, not to deny its even more crucial relationship to West African musical forms and traditions.

"Fragile" because throughout most of jazz's now more or less 100-year history, classical music and jazz have been rejecting each other, misinterpreting each other, mistrusting each other, and frequently skimming off the top elements and concepts indigenous to both traditions in ways that can only be described as superficial. "Confusing and misinterpreted" because of ignorance and prejudice

9

on both sides—although I hasten to add that in the realm of prejudice, classical music and musicians have the longer and sadder history.

In these relatively few words, I believe I have staked out the territory, the frame of reference, in which our discussion must take place; but to lay out the territory is not yet to define the territory. We must take care of that detail before we tackle the larger question of jazz's influence on classical music.

First, let us dispose of some annoying questions of terminology and mythology. The language with which we describe these two musics is inaccurate and confusing. The word "jazz" is and was an indignity that most thinking individuals by now reject as a proper name for America's one truly indigenous musical art form. It persists, of course, both by traditional long-term usage and for lack of a handy or more appropriate term.

"Classical" and "concert music" are also inaccurate and severely limiting terms. Even within the realm of so-called "classical music," the term is used differently by its own practitioners. Some use the term generically to describe all music that comes out of the Western art tradition, a definition that leaves folk, popular, ethnic, or vernacular European musical traditions in terminological limbo. Historians and musicologists limit the term "classical" to a specific period in European musical history, the years roughly between 1750 and 1825.

To add further confusion to the semantic muddle, many jazz writers and critics have lately begun to call jazz "America's classical music" while others refer to the 1930s, the Swing Era, as the "classical" period in jazz. Those who apply the term "classical" to jazz or to some of its developments are undoubtedly well-meaning, though misguided. Their thinking is based on the most ancient of myths: In order to gain acceptance in our society and musical culture, jazz needs the approbation of borrowed European aesthetic terminology. Jazz is its own self-defining musical art form. It does not or would not, in a world of justice and understanding, need to defend its pedigree or its right of existence in terms other than its own.

"Concert music" is an even more confusing and limiting term. On the one hand, not all "classical" Western music is performed in concert. Nor can it be said that jazz is not played in concerts. Benny Goodman's 1938 Carnegie Hall concert, Duke Ellington's years of Carnegie appearances, and Norman Granz's "Jazz at the Philharmonic" took care of that syndrome a long time ago.

Let us gratefully note, however, that we have at least finally done away with the term "serious music"—as if jazz were an unserious music—and that the rest of the musical field has not done much better with terminology. For example, "popular music" (in which jazz is often included) means, to some people, music that has attained popular success, with the emphasis on success and a further emphasis on financial success. To others popular music means music of the people, by the people, for the people, something akin to folk music. But does folk music still really exist? Indeed, are there any "folk" left in this world of instant electronic communication, in which the isolation that used to spawn folkloric, ethnic, regional, and national traditions has all but disappeared? Today's so-called folk music is a synthetic, inauthentic product primarily conceived in the Brill building and in Nashville recording studios.

That is why the term "vernacular music" is more appropriate. At least it is a more harmless term, avoiding all the complex implications of popularity or of authenticity. By the same token, names like "rock music" and "third stream" also have the virtue of a modicum of descriptive accuracy. They at least say more or less what they are, and in themselves do not cause confusion—which is not to say, alas, that they are not often misunderstood or misinterpreted.

This imperfect terminology makes the task of defining what we are talking about all the more difficult. Even the terms "improvised music" and "black music" are inadequate for jazz, for not all jazz is improvised, and many other musics besides jazz are improvised. Not all jazz is black, either, although clearly its origin is black, its essence is black, and all of its major creative thrusts have come from black musicians.

As for the aforementioned question of myths—and for the purpose of this discussion, I would like to single out only one of the many myths surrounding jazz—jazz has always seemed expected to measure and defend itself against the prevailing white, essentially European, establishments and concepts of music. If we are going to discuss the influence of jazz on the history and development of concert music, that is, classical music, then I for one can only carry on that discussion in terms of artistic and social equality. Jazz is a music as capable of greatness as any other musical tradition. Jazz can claim its own venerable traditions and distinctive artistic accomplishments. It can even be argued that jazz and its derivatives have exerted a more powerful, penetrating, worldwide influence than any other music in human history. The fact that jazz is loved, understood, studied, and taken seriously everywhere in the world except in the land of its origin is, of course, a tragic reality. This is a reality that many of us, including the National Jazz Service Organization, hope to amend.

The sad truth is that jazz is one of America's most neglected musics, particularly in its more modern and advanced manifestations. If the average American recognizes the existence of jazz at all, he is likely to think of the music called Dixieland, or even worse, such pallid commercial derivatives as the music of Lawrence Welk or Guy Lombardo. Even in more enlightened circles, jazz is reluctantly accepted in patronizing condescension as mere functional music, for dancing, for example; a mere entertainment music with its creative, artistic, and aesthetic merits ignored.

I do not wish to imply that functional music is a demeaning category. The adjective "mere" is added by those who see jazz only as a commercial, usable, buyable, exploitable entertainment commodity. In its earlier history and development from a true black folk music through a nationally popular entertainment music to a world art music, jazz was indeed primarily a dance music, and proud of it. It derived much of its strength and sustenance from being a dance music. But jazz has long ago moved beyond the realm of dance and entertainment functions, those being limitations not inherent to the deeper nature of jazz.

The patronization of jazz has its origins in its social history. For deep-rooted social, political, and economic reasons, jazz was born on the wrong side of the tracks as far as the prevailing white-dominated society was concerned. The fact that society imposed the very conditions that did not permit jazz to be born on the right side of the tracks did not occur to those who condemned jazz for its lowly and unacceptable origins. Ignoring the realities of poverty, illiteracy, and prejudice made it easier to denigrate and ignore the music. Alas, this vicious circle has not been entirely broken even to this day.

How all the more glorious it is that the music we call jazz has triumphed over all these trials, tribulations, and vicissitudes, whether it be its humble birth, its rejection by its own homeland, or its near demise in the 1970s at the hands of rock and roll, ironically one of its own ungrateful and greedy offsprings. In fact it would not be difficult for a social historian to argue that much of jazz's strength and persistence derives from its ceaseless battle with opposition and neglect, and its constant confrontation with impossible odds. Indeed, its very birth and existence derive from its creators' deprived place in our history and society. What an irony in all this!

The question as to the influence of jazz and classical music upon each other was often asked in the past with the automatic implication that jazz needs to justify itself and be measured vis-à-vis classical music. Twenty-five years ago, when controversy raged over the concept and name of third stream, the assumption on both sides was that the idea behind third stream was to bring jazz up to the level of classical music, that jazz somehow needed infusion from the classical side to be a music that could be taken seriously. I can vouch for the fact that that was not what I intended when I coined the third-stream idea. The arguments were symptomatic of the unease that existed on both sides: that somehow each music would be contaminated by contact with the other.

The conservatives on the jazz side wanted to preserve jazz from further musical and technical advances: bebop and modern jazz, according to them, had already done enough damage along those lines. Jazz progressives, on the other hand, wanted to preserve jazz from what they called the further intellectualization and academicization of jazz, robbing it—so they alleged—of its freedom and spontaneity. The special irony in this was that many of these self-styled progressives had almost driven jazz to the brink of atrophy by their virtual elimination of improvisation.

On the other side, classical composers, critics, pundits, and purists saw the contact with jazz not so much as dangerous as irrelevant, and beneath classical music's dignity. This attitude harked back to that old bromide held by many in the classical field: "Jazz is all right in its place, but what is it doing in Symphony Hall?"

The storm raised by the concept of third stream was but one brief cloudburst in a long, ongoing history of coexistence and cross-fertilization between jazz music and concert music. Contrary to its adversaries' claims, third stream was not touted as something new, nor as some panacea to contemporary music's problems, and least of all as a musical form that was going to replace both jazz and classical music. The idea embedded in the basic philosophy of third stream was its concept of an offspring begotten from the marriage of two equal mainstreams—and I emphasize the word "equal." These two musics could also be left to continue to develop in their own organic ways without benefit of further fusion if they so chose; that is, to remain discreet and distinct. Today the third stream is but one approach by which the two musics can find and meet each other on common ground.

The history of cross-fertilization goes back to the very beginnings of jazz. To the extent that African musical traditions were allowed to survive in America through slavery and the early decades of emancipation, and began to merge and integrate with the European musical tradition, some rare individuals on the classical side, with their ears to the ground, began to take note of what was emerging in black and Indian folklore. The most famous and influential of these were Antonín Dvořák and Charles Ives: Dvořák urging his American students and colleagues to use native folk or popular materials in their music, and Ives actually borrowing and incorporating the rhythms and new spirit of black ragtime in his works as early as 1901. It is interesting to envision Jelly Roll Morton listening to opera and other classical music in the French Opera House in New Orleans and to the brass and woodwind bands that played in the parks and on the riverboats in those days, and Ives, 1,500 miles away, listening to ragtime orchestras in the Globe Theatre in New Haven or in other places of entertainment in New York and Danbury.

In Denver black violinist George Morrison was studying classical music, even taking lessons from the renowned Fritz Kreisler while working as a musician in Denver honky-tonks; at almost the same time, one of his teachers, Wilberforce Whiteman (who also taught Andy Kirk and Mary Colston the fundamentals of music), was sympathetically listening to the emerging music of jazz, encouraging his son, Paul, to enter that field rather than play viola in the Denver Symphony.

Picture Scott Joplin composing his great classic rags, borrowing the basic ragtime form from John Philip Sousa's marches and learning proper harmony and theory from other classical sources, then Sousa returning the compliment by taking ragtime to Europe as early as 1900 and frequently defending it to its legions of detractors. Indeed it was Sousa who first brought ragtime to the attention of composers like Debussy and Satie. Following later were James Europe's recordings and performances (particularly with his Hell Fighters Band) and by Will Marion Cook's Southern Syncopated Orchestra, a group that toured Europe in 1919 and drew the first intelligent criticism of what might legitimately be called jazz from the young Swiss musician Ernest Ansermet, a close friend of Stravinsky.

By the late teens of the century, when ragtime was just being transformed into jazz, Stravinsky had written several ragtime pieces: a short dance sequence in *Histoire du soldat*, a piano piece, and a work called *Ragtime* for eleven instruments, featuring the unjazz-like Hungarian national instrument, the cimbalom. While Debussy's, Satie's, and Ives's works easily captured the style and essential characteristics of ragtime, Stravinsky's barely did. At times Stravinsky's early jazz pieces are almost as remote from ragtime as his *Ebony Concerto* of 1943 is from jazz; but remoteness from their avowed source does not necessarily make them works of lesser creativity or of lesser skill and quality. I do not think it was a matter of incompetence in adopting the new American style, but rather one of choice. Stravinsky seems to have been unwilling to relinquish as much of himself and his then rather acerbic, sparse musical language as were Debussy and Satie of theirs.

Indeed, more than any others, Stravinsky's jazz and ragtime works raise the question of how one should evaluate the artistic merit of such hybrid efforts. Are we to evaluate them by their stylistic authenticity to the sources they claim to have been inspired by, or are we to evaluate them on their own terms and merits as finite works, regardless of stylistic pedigrees? In other words, how important is the ragginess of Stravinsky's *Ragtime* or the jazziness of his *Ebony Concerto*? It is the same question that folklorists might have asked Mozart regarding the authenticity of the minuets in his symphonies, or of Bach's sarabandes in his suites. It is still the central question when we encounter works announcing that they are based, to some extent, on a popular or vernacular style.

Though we tend nowadays to accept the integrity and unity of Bartók's use of Hungarian and Romanian folk material, I can well imagine that fifty years ago aficionados of Hungarian folk and dance music could relate more positively to Bartók's simpler folk-influenced works than they could, say, to his complex, harshly dissonant *Miraculous Mandarin* ballet music. Conversely, I can also imagine that in those early days certain Balkan ethnomusicological purists must have resented the intrusion of atonal and modern harmonics into the private domain of their folkloric territory. The question arises time and time again when we confront jazz-influenced classical works (as well as those on the jazz side that borrowed elements from the classical field).

With the mention of Stravinsky's works, we had arrived at a time coincident with the very beginnings of jazz. As jazz and blues, suddenly widely disseminated through recordings, spread like wildfire, composers everywhere began to be captivated by jazz and its novel sounds. Some of the more important composers who were attracted to the upstart mavericks from the wrong side of the tracks included, in this country, John Alden Carpenter, George Gershwin, Aaron Copland, and Louis Gruenberg; and in Europe, Darius Milhaud,

Maurice Ravel, Arthur Honegger, Georges Auric, William Walton, Alfredo Casella, Paul Hindemith, Ernst Krenek, Kurt Weill, and <u>Boris Blacher</u>, to name some. Very few of them, however, captured the true spirit of jazz, or even wanted to. There is a good reason for that: very few of them ever heard true jazz. Most of them heard the more commercial trivializations of jazz, as purveyed on popular recordings or as heard in transplanted dance orchestras—with their token "hot" musicians playing an occasional "hot" chorus —in the finer hotels of Paris, Berlin, and London. They did not hear the Hot Five recordings of Louis Armstrong, the early recordings of Ellington and Henderson, the Savoy Bearcats, or Charlie Johnson's Paradise Band.

What all those composers, with one exception, failed to hear and see was that true jazz was an essentially improvised, spontaneously created music. Aaron Copland, for one, admitted years after the fact that he was exclusively interested in the jaunty, perky, syncopated rhythms of jazz; its fascinating sounds and timbres; its newfangled brass mutes; and its effects (like the trombone glissando, the growl, and so on). The fact that these rhythms and effects were the result of a confrontation between divergent cultures and musical traditions seems to have held little interest for Copland and his contemporaries.

The one exception was Milhaud, who did hear authentic black jazz in 1922 in Harlem and in Georgia. While on a U.S. visit to conduct the Philadelphia Orchestra at the invitation of Leopold Stokowski, he went with friends to hear "le jazz hot" in Harlem. He also brought back to France a stack of records he bought in Harlem, mostly on the Black Swan and Gennett labels (in those days called race records) of artists such as Fletcher Henderson, Ethel Waters, King Oliver, and the New Orleans Rhythm Kings. The result of his encounter with real jazz was his 1923 *La Création du monde,* a work that, without relinquishing any aspect of Milhaud's own already well-formed bitonal and polytonal style, captures the spirit and freedom of spontaneity, and the polymetric, polyphonic essence of early jazz more than any other "classical" work known to me.

How close Milhaud came to capturing the spirit, sound, and excitement of early jazz can be gained by comparing certain excerpts from

La Création du monde (the Fugue, for example) with excerpts from the Original Dixieland Jazz Band's *Livery Stable Blues,* a 1917 recording that all European intellectuals knew by 1920 and live performances of which many had heard on the Original Dixieland Jazz Band's 1918 European tour.

My point about Milhaud's identification with black jazz is not weakened by the fact that the Original Dixieland Jazz Band was a white band. First, it was a band that seriously tried to emulate its black New Orleans counterparts. Second, the Original Dixieland Jazz Band did feature a particularly abandoned, raucous, almost uncultivated boisterousness that must have appealed to a sophisticated, rebellious Parisian like Milhaud. Third, I suspect that the Gennett and Black Swan recordings Milhaud bought were of such poor technical quality, as compared to the state-of-the-art Victor recordings, that the Original Dixieland Jazz Band's record served as a much more accessible and audible model to emulate.

But by the early 1930s, the novelty of jazz had begun to wear off for European and American composers. Its attraction as a source of inspiration, even in a superficial sense, had begun to wane, especially in the face of the extraordinary advances taking place harmonically, rhythmically, structurally, technically—in short, linguistically—in contemporary music. Against Schoenberg's freely atonal works of the teens and 20s, and his twelve-tone works of the late 20s; against Stravinsky's highly sophisticated neoclassicism of the 20s and 30s; against the experiments of the Antheils, the Ornsteins, the Sorabjis, the Henry Cowells; against the Young Turks in Europe like Igor Markevich, Webern, and Berg; and against Shostakovich and Prokofiev in Russia, jazz of the late 20s and early 30s began to seem—to classical composers—rather primitive, limited, repetitious, and devoid of radical invention. The last major works of that era that reflected the earlier fascination with jazz were Louis Gruenberg's *Jazz Suite for Orchestra* of 1930, Ravel's two piano concertos, and Honegger's 1930 concertos for cello and for piano.

It is amazing that all those composers did not hear or listen to Ellington's *Mood Indigo, Daybreak Express,* or *Creole Rhapsody;* Fletcher

Henderson's *King Porter Stomp* or *Queer Notions;* Bennie Moten's *Toby* and *Prince of Wails;* Chick Webb's *Dog Bottom;* Jimmy Lunceford's *Jazznocracy;* or even the Casa Loma's *Casa Loma Stomp.* In effect, they shut off the jazz spigot and the result was a long dry spell for the compositional influence of jazz on classical music. It was a dry spell that continued well into the late 40s.

Interestingly enough, the fascination with and attraction to jazz began to be felt in an entirely different realm, that of instrumental technique, especially brass and wind. To the utter amazement of conservatory-trained classical musicians, the mostly untutored jazz musicians had, out of their own resources, energies, and instincts, taken instruments such as the trumpet, the trombone, the clarinet, and especially the saxophone, and enormously expanded their technical and expressive boundaries. Louis Armstrong, Jabbo Smith, Rex Stewart, and Cootie Williams could do on their trumpets and cornets what no symphony trumpet player could even dream of doing, let alone carry out, certainly not in spontaneous improvisations. Lawrence Brown, Jimmy Harrison, "Tricky Sam" Nanton, Tommy Dorsey, and Jack Teagarden could perform on their trombones feats of dexterity, agility, endurance, and expressive versatility that no trombonist in the New York or Berlin Philharmonics could imagine, let alone duplicate. I won't mention what happened to the clarinet with Benny Goodman and Jimmie Noone; to the saxophone with Coleman Hawkins and Ben Webster; and to percussion with Chick Webb, Gene Krupa, and Sid Catlett.

In the realm of brass instrumental range, jazz musicians led the way and broke all existing boundaries. Schoenberg wrote one high E-flat for trumpet in his *Orchestra Variations* of 1928 (and he made that optional), and Stravinsky wrote one in 1913 in his *Rite of Spring* (but that was for the smaller, narrow-bored, newly invented piccolo trumpet); but when Louis Armstrong started hitting high Fs regularly in the early 30s—one night in Paris in 1933 he played seventy successive high Cs in one song—it was hard for classical players to argue that such high notes couldn't be played on the trumpet. They could no longer ignore the reality of Armstrong's awesome achievement and justify their indolence by the fact that trumpet exercise books contained no high Fs.

The same was true for the trombone: Trummy Young's and Jack Jenney's mid-30s high Fs, played with consummate ease and used for expressive, not pyrotechnical, purposes, led eventually to the extraordinary trombonistic exploits of Bill Harris, Urbie Green, Bill Watrous, Jimmy Cleveland, and Curtis Fuller.

Combine these advances with the invention and expressive use of the cup mute, the Harmon mute, the megaphone mute, and the bathroom plunger in an evolution of an entirely new sound spectrum for the saxophone by Coleman Hawkins, Lester Young, Johnny Hodges, John Coltrane, and Ornette Coleman, and you begin to gain a glimpse of similar technical and expressive extensions jazz players have brought to their instruments and to music.

Through the decades, the extraordinary advances made by jazz players have gradually trickled down to the classical field. While most classical players still cannot cope with the full extent of the jazz players' self-created demands, there is at least now a wide-eyed respect for jazz players and a dramatic expansion of the technical skills of classical wind players and percussionists. The days when Dizzy Gillespie's high-flying trumpet parts could only be played by classical flutists are finally gone.

Paradoxically, it was the expanded skills of American brass and woodwind players that brought composers back to jazz in the middle and late 40s, a development that continues to grow. Whether in some of the works of Leonard Bernstein, Gunther Schuller, William Russo, Alec Wilder, Hall Overton, Bill Smith, André Hodeir, David Baker, Anthony Davis, or James Newton, the integration of jazz styles and jazz techniques led eventually in recent years to a true synthesis of styles and musical concepts. Boundaries between jazz and classical music are often so blurred as to be no longer discernible. The avant-garde in both fields have met, embraced, and fructified in ways that defy labeling and categorizing, one hopes precluding the terminological confusion I mentioned earlier. The distance (in broad linguistic terms) between the pianism of a Cecil Taylor or a Ran Blake and the pianism of an Elliott Carter or a Milton Babbitt is not all that great. The recent scores of Bob Brookmeyer or Carla Bley are not all that different from countless scores of the European and American classical avant-garde. And who is to say whether the music of James Newton, Anthony Davis, Anthony Braxton, Leo Smith, and David Baker belong in the classical or jazz field?

This brings us right back to the question raised by the early Stravinsky and Milhaud works, a question that is still with us today: By what criteria shall we evaluate such works? Is it on their intrinsic values as compositions, regardless of their stylistic persuasion? How much do the thoroughness of fusion and the quality of the elements being fused enter into an evaluation of the work under consideration?

These are difficult questions. In the arts no absolute, completely objective, finite, demonstrable judgments are possible. At best all we have are presumably enlightened, informed, well-considered opinions in which we can hope that stylistic preconceptions and prejudgments will be largely absent. Still, there are two ways to answer those questions. The first is to judge the work on its own merits, based on its own purported intentions as far as we can know them as indicated by the composer (or improviser) or from a thorough study of the work itself. Second, and perhaps even more important, is the factor of performance quality and authenticity. This is especially true when improvisation or any specific, easily recognizable stylistic element is involved. Many times works that represent stylistic crossbreeding have been unfairly criticized for compositional and conceptual failings, when in fact it was their performances that were crucially flawed. Milhaud's *Création du monde* has frequently been criticized by jazz critics because it didn't swing, because its jazz elements didn't sound spontaneous. In Milhaud's first recording of the work in the late 20s, played by French non-jazz studio musicians, of course it didn't swing; it couldn't have. Those musicians couldn't play jazz, nor could real jazz musicians of that time have read and performed that score. Today, sixty years later, any number of musicians can render authentically all aspects of that great work, at least in the seventeen-piece chamber version.

Similarly, Stravinsky's *Ebony Concerto* could not be played correctly and authentically by the Woody Herman Band at its premiere in 1943, and yet the work was roundly condemned by classical critics who could not recognize that the performers fell short of the task. In that instance the jazz critics also were disappointed, because they could not comprehend the nonjazz elements and character of the work. Nor could those critics hear that the musicians in Herman's band, dealing with a difficult, completely written-out score, were unable to do justice to the jazz elements it did contain.

No hybrid work should be judged until it has been performed authentically, giving the work its full due as required by the stylistic amalgams contained therein. Only then can one deal somewhat objectively with the work as a whole. The degree to which a work respects the stylistic components it proposes to merge is less important than the imagination or creativity with which those elements are fused. It is the newness, the originality that results from the fusion that counts, not mere novelty or experimentation for experimentation's sake.

It seems to me quite irrelevant whether a jazz-influenced work makes use of this or that style of jazz or this or that classical concept or technique. It does matter that what takes place is a true fusion, not some superficial overlay of one part of the amalgam on the other, a mere veneer. Some new, heretofore unattainable creative result should evolve from this marriage. That, by the way, happens also to have been the underlying concept of third stream as I originally envisioned it.

By such criteria, the degree to which a jazz-influenced or third-stream work succeeds or fails is not measurable by the degree to which the composer or creators succeed in fully representing the various stylistic elements. It is rather the degree to which a work brings forth a new totality, never heard of before, that counts. To the extent that one element inspires, informs, and fructifies the other, it makes the work more successful artistically, regardless of its stylistic pedigree.

Seen from this viewpoint, the influence of jazz on certain composers, on certain 20th-century works, and on certain developments in contemporary music has been, on the whole, positive and benign, at the very least instructive. A rich body of work now exists that could not have been written without the benefit of jazz, a body of work that represents one important direction the synthesis of various elements, styles, and languages has taken in our century. To me, as an American, it is one of the most fascinating and relevant syntheses to occur in our time, although to a Hungarian national, Bartók's work with Hungarian folk music might seem more important and more relevant.

Such are the variations possible in our present-day musical environment, where the world's musics, in all their myriad disparateness, come closer together. The results, I suppose, in some faraway future will be the ultimate grand synthesis, in which all musics coexist peacefully and even cohabit fruitfully. The entire history of music, particularly European music, is, like the genetic process itself, a prolonged history of musical intermarriage, acculturation, crossbreeding, fusing, and new symbiotic relationships, always subject to further renewal and genetic regeneration.

What we have witnessed thus far in the influence of jazz upon classical music is but a small flick on the larger screen of history, and we have just arrived at one of the many new beginnings. The energizing force of jazz has already contributed a great deal, but I am certain there is much more to come.

Olly Wilson, *Respondent*

The Influence of Jazz on the History and Development of Concert Music

Gunther Schuller has provided us with an informative, perceptive, and provocative paper. As is the case with his work in general, the paper is enlivened by a breadth of knowledge, a keen sense of aesthetic taste, and a sensitivity to the subtleties and nuances of a complex issue.

This is not to say that I concur with everything put forward in the paper. Such unanimity would suggest an astounding degree of conformity, given the complexity of the issue before us. Nevertheless, on a fundamental level, I concur with Schuller's basic premises.

First, that "the relationship between jazz and classical 'concert music' has always been both profound and fragile, and frequently confusing and misinterpreted." Second, that "jazz is its own self-defining musical art form [that] does not or would not, in a world of justice and understanding, need to defend its pedigree or its right of existence in terms other than its own." Hence, the title of the paper is somewhat bothersome. It implies in a subtle way that jazz is important only because of its influence on the development of "concert music," rather than on its own merit.

Schuller's third premise is that an individual work of one tradition that is influenced in either superficial or significant ways by another musical tradition must be judged on its own merits rather than the degree that it reflects the sensibilities of that second tradition. This approach assumes that the work is performed in a manner consistent with its creator's intent.

The picture that Schuller paints is one of coexisting major artistic traditions that inevitably impact on one another at different times, to different degrees, with varying results. Of significant interest is Schuller's discussion of the ambiguities and inadequacies of terms like "jazz," "concert music," and "classical music." It is important to remind ourselves of the limitations and biases inherent in these terms. They reflect a confusion of thought, a distorted view of reality. The persistence and pervasiveness of that "most ancient of myths, [that jazz,] in order to gain acceptance in our society and musical culture, needs the approbation of borrowed European aesthetic terminology" are clear reflections of fundamental misconceptions about the nature of Afro-American music.

That myth is a reflection of a cultural ethnocentric assumption that has been firmly rooted in the conventional wisdom of American society. The assumption is that there is a single, dominant, musical tradition, spawned by post-Renaissance developments in Western Europe, that represents the zenith of creation in the field of music. All other music must be compared to and measured against that tradition. Because of this assumption, most Western musical criticism, whether on a scholarly or journalistic level, has ignored, patronized, or condemned the rich musical practices that existed alongside the "classical" Western tradition, either from within that tradition (the "so-called" folk and popular realms) or from without (the music of non-Western cultures).

The very nature of standard Western discourse about music (all too often taken as the only possible discourse) reflects this bias. Students of non-Western traditions quickly learn that concepts such as harmony, melody, and rhythm may have very different meanings when applied to non-Western music. They learn that the act of making music in some cultures is inclusive of some behavioral pattern extrinsic to music making in the West, but exclusive of others. The point here is that the terminology we use is often based on assumptions held by a specific Western music tradition. Obviously, the recognition of this problem is the first step toward solving it.

The basic assumption of the centrality of the Western European literate musical tradition also affects the tradition called jazz in other fundamental ways. Schuller states that "the fact that jazz is loved, understood, studied, and taken seriously everywhere in the world except in the land of its origin is . . . a tragic reality." I would suggest that a direct correlation exists between the seriousness with which an art is taken and the level of support it enjoys from those institutions in this society that traditionally support art. If, consciously or unconsciously, one views the Western European literate musical tradition as central, then in a world of conflicting priorities, that tradition will enjoy a special status in the academy, corporate boardrooms, foundations, and the government. It thus becomes incumbent upon those of us who reject such cultural Darwinism to challenge the misconception of the superiority and centrality of Western European music.

This is not to deny the significance and importance of the Western European literate musical tradition, whose glory speaks for itself. It is simply to view that tradition within a broader perspective that takes into consideration the reality of equally significant traditions. That broader perspective is essential to understanding our present reality and affecting the future. Basic assumptions and collectively shared ideas about the nature of reality do have a direct impact on human behavior. Jazz will never be accorded the respect and support it deserves until basic misconceptions about its nature are expunged from our national consciousness. I'm sure this is a major part of the agenda of the National Jazz Service Organization.

Schuller understands these issues, and he has discussed the influence of jazz on concert music in terms of the artistic equality of the two traditions. He presents us with a chronological overview of the nature of this relationship, beginning with the impact of Afro-American music on Dvorák and Ives in the last decade of the 19th century, and continuing with the reciprocal influences of Joplin and Sousa on one another and the subsequent influences of ragtime on Debussy and Satie. He then discusses the irony of the 1920s, a decade that, in spite of the profusion of American and European composers of the "written tradition" who ostensibly were influenced by jazz, produced very little music by these composers reflecting more than a superficial knowledge of jazz.

Finally, after reviewing the waning of the jazz influence in the 30s, he discusses the role of jazz performance techniques as a major influence on composers outside of that tradition in the 40s, 50s, and 60s. He sees "third-stream music" as a logical outgrowth of the historical interaction of these two coequal traditions—not as something that juxtaposes opposing musical impulses or subsumes one tradition under the other, but rather as a fusion of both traditions in which some "new, heretofore unattainable creative result should evolve."

Within this overview of the influence of jazz on concert music, Schuller has cited examples of both profound relationships as well as fragile ones. I would like to expand on this theme as well as Schuller's statement that he views the essence of jazz as black. I view both ragtime and jazz as part of an Afro-American musical tradition, which is itself an outgrowth of a larger West African musical tradition. Time does not permit a thorough discussion of the nature of the relationship of West African to Afro-American music, but it may be summarized as the common sharing of a critical core of conceptual approaches to the process of music making. By this, I mean that certain basic ways of approaching the musical process, and certain fundamental notions about the basic nature of music, are reflected in specific, demonstrable characteristics of the music. For example:

• the approach to the organization of rhythm based on the principle of rhythmic contrast;

• the assumption that the musical process is a communal one that presumes the active participation in varying degrees of a communion of participants;

• the tendency to regard physical body motion as an integral part of the music-making process;

• the approach to singing or the playing of any instrument in a percussive manner;

• the tendency to use a wide range of dramatically contrasting musical timbres (qualities of sound) in both vocal and instrumental music;

• the tendency to create call-and-response musical structures on a multitude of structural levels.

The particular genres of Afro-American music that have evolved in the United States are specific realizations of this conceptual framework and also reflections of specific experiences. As such, the common core uniting the broader West African–based tradition consists of common ways of doing things, although the specific qualities of the something that is done varies with time and place and is also influenced by a number of elements outside the tradition. Therefore, in any particular Afro-American musical genre, one would expect to find a reflection of these basic characteristics.

Given the above perspective, it becomes possible to see the relationship of Euro-American written tradition to Afro-American tradition in a slightly different light. I agree with Schuller that the influence of jazz on concert music has been profound, as well as fragile. I suggest, further, that the relationship is considered profound to the extent that a fundamental component of that basic conceptual core has been internalized by the Euro-American tradition.

What makes Milhaud's *Création du monde* swing is that it manages to project rhythmic contrast and timbral differentiation convincingly in Afro-American terms. Milhaud captured a fundamental quality of that tradition while maintaining the integrity of his own artistic vision. In the same sense, what makes the influence of jazz performance techniques on contemporary music of the 50s and particularly the 60s profound is the fact that the new virtuosity and the extended instrumental and vocal techniques of the most exciting contemporary music of that period—the vocal style of Berio's *Circles,* for example—reflect an influence that occurs at the conceptual level. Such music is based on a different approach to producing sound from an instrument or voice, and in some instances it looks toward a different model for timbral relationships between instruments. It is in this same sense that African and Afro-American concepts of group improvisation, multi-layering of musical textures, and nonteleological concepts of musical time have had an important impact on the development of such ideas as indeterminacy and open-ended musical form.

Conversely, those works that show only a superficial influence of jazz do so because they are not affected by the tradition at a conceptual level. The use of a muted trumpet or a perky syncopated rhythm, which characterized much of the written music of the 20s, is simply a surface feature that did not affect the composer's essential musical conception.

In order for an influence from one musical tradition to significantly affect the development of another musical tradition, it must modify that second tradition's view of itself at a conceptual level. It must propagate a significantly altered ordering of itself—a new paradigm.

Schuller closes his paper with an optimistic prognosis for the future. He sees the experience of the relationship of jazz and concert music as perhaps a harbinger of greater interaction among various music cultures, as the world develops greater awareness of the full range of its human diversity—an inevitable consequence of the technological, geopolitical, and social forces that inexorably move humanity toward global interdependence. He describes an ultimate grand synthesis in which all musical traditions "coexist peacefully and fruitfully."

I share that optimism, but I don't envision, nor does Schuller suggest, the ultimate emergence of a preeminent musical tradition as the result of the intermingling of various traditions. I see rather the simultaneous existence of multiple traditions that are fruitfully influenced by one another, occasionally bringing into existence new traditions, but for the most part developing along lines that retain their essential qualities—qualities that reflect basic conceptions. I find Schuller's point in his discussion of Stravinsky's *Ragtime* particularly instructive; clearly this work could not have been written without Stravinsky having experienced, even in a diluted form, the ragtime and early jazz tradition.

The same observation is probably true of several works or sections of works by Stravinsky—the last movement of the *Octet*, for example. Nevertheless, these pieces are more Stravinsky than ragtime. In a similar sense, Charlie Parker was conversant with much of the written contemporary music of his time, and he, like many of his generation, occasionally quoted themes from the written classical tradition in his improvisation; but obviously the abiding strength of his conception was not dependent on these quotes, or the addition of a large string orchestra to his ensemble. These additions were superficial to his basic language.

What we have witnessed so far from the influence of jazz upon classical music is indeed a "small flick on the larger screen of history." But it is an influence that increases exponentially as we face the future. The energizing force of jazz will continue to spawn offspring, both profound and superficial, as it simultaneously reconfigures itself and continues its vital enrichment of our lives.

Gary Giddins, *Presenter*

The Evolution of Jazz

William Hazlitt suggested that every art achieves its highest plateau in infancy. Certainly this would seem true of jazz. Louis Armstrong's music embodied a conceptual power and a technical finesse that the whole world found irresistible. Yet the sublimity of his triumph was marred from the beginning by assumptions about what an artist ought to be and how art itself ought to function. Since those assumptions were largely rooted in the prejudices of 19th-century European romanticism, and in the Puritanism and self-abasement that are rampant in American culture, they might be characterized as misguided and provincial at best and as Philistine and racist at worst. They haunted Armstrong throughout his career and they haunt jazz today. One reproof that jazz critics frequently lobbed at him concerned his alleged willingness to compromise. In balancing the priorities of his art against the demands of a mass audience, he is said to have discredited his music. That accusation gets to the heart of jazz's evolution, since not even in its most insular stage did it evolve in a vacuum. On the contrary, jazz evolved as part of an equilateral triangle along with the traditions of the academy ("classical" music) and the marketplace ("pop" music).

I suspect that, as the supreme artist of jazz's infancy, Armstrong might have found the notion of compromise—in the sense of calculating dilution—unfathomable. After all, it was his fate to take jazz out of the woods and spread it around the globe. Like any good missionary, he must have reveled in every convert he made, and he surely understood that the magnificence of his art transcended the barriers his detractors sought to bolster. Here was a singer who did not have a singer's voice, by bel canto or pop standards. Here was a trumpet player, composer, and bandleader without an academic background, a learned grasp of theory, or a conservatory technique. Armstrong was, in a real sense, his own academy. He surely realized, if few others did, that his homemade music was equal in strength to any other. He was nonetheless accused of violating traditions that, had they been perpetuated, could only have guaranteed jazz the status, audience, and interest of a folk or guild music. Was it a compromise for him to sing *Body and Soul* in addition to *Muskrat Ramble?* Was it a compromise for him to take his talent and appeal into various corners of the entertainment world, from Betty Boop cartoons to symphonic concertos, from vaudeville to radio to television, from the service of spirituals to that of Walt Disney themes? One might as well dismiss opera buffa for its dependency on low farce. How strange that complaints are registered because Armstrong refused to shackle his genius with high-minded conventions to please the intelligentsia, especially when the intelligentsia took no real pleasure in Armstrong.

I invoke Armstrong specifically, but also to represent the generation of musicians that produced Duke Ellington, Jelly Roll Morton, Sidney Bechet, Bessie Smith, and Coleman Hawkins, among others who produced innovative, enduring art while sampling the benefits and pressures of the pop marketplace. Aside from individual masterpieces, their collective contribution to the evolution of music has been the equilateral triangle I mentioned. Before jazz, there was no triangle—only a line, a rope if you will, tugged on one side by the forces of high art and on the other by the forces of low. Afro-American music, of which jazz is the most accomplished, ambitious, and inclusive expression, altered cultural geometry. The achievement of black music has made the 20th century the American century in music, as surely as the 19th century was musically Germanic. Jazz, blues, rags, dixie, swing, bop, the new thing, rhythm and blues, rock and roll, disco, and rap—these are some of the labels that have grown out of the Afro-American approach to the conception and execution of music. But unlike most of those terms, which often signify musical fashions dependent on the marketplace, jazz has evolved separately according to its own inner lights. In other words, it has behaved like a classical music, even though it briefly enjoyed—as European classical music briefly enjoyed—the advantages of popular acclamation.

We who study and enjoy jazz are often beset with qualms that so many opportunities were missed. Why didn't Ellington or Gil Evans write concertos for Armstrong? Why wasn't Armstrong taken from the familiar context of his All Stars groups of the 1950s and 60s and encouraged to perform with his successors—Eldridge, Gillespie, and especially Miles Davis, who brought some of Armstrong's licks into modernism? The fact that we ask such questions belies a lingering sentimentality in our appreciation of this young music. For we know the answers. We know that Armstrong made better records with his own All Stars than with the modernist Esquire All-Stars, just as he made better records with the Mills Brothers than with Oscar Peterson. We don't really believe that Armstrong and Davis would have wrought magic of unimaginable dimensions if brought together, yet the image of father and son united on stage is strangely comforting, particularly in light of jazz's speedy evolution. It helps us convince ourselves that their music is homogeneous—a singular form you can put a hat on and call jazz.

Armstrong, who said "Jazz is only what you are," knew better, as did Ellington, who said "I don't know how such great extremes as now exist can be contained under the one heading." We're tempted to think that because jazz's greatest figures—from Jelly Roll Morton to Cecil Taylor—were born within a period of forty years that differences in style are less substantive than they appear. We are stymied by the rapidity with which jazz has developed from a functional music (fulfilling the needs of its audience) to a modernist art (which by definition rejects the conventions and expectations of its audience) to various postmodernist movements that reject the expectations not only of the bourgeoisie, but of musicians and critics as well. By the time the avant-garde took hold, other functional pop musics had long since displaced jazz, leaving it the enviable freedom to test and relearn its original intentions.

No one should be surprised that the jazz audience is now a small but loyal coterie of the sort that sticks to an art after the art has been abandoned by—or has abandoned (it's a two-way street)—the larger audience. The central issue that confronts jazz today isn't tradition versus modernism, but art versus pop, for that conflict contains the seed for the most pressing issue of all: appreciation versus neglect. If jazz is construed as a pop art, then its failure in the marketplace is a just epitaph, and society has no obligation to ensure its survival. But if we recognize jazz as the art it is—as a pleasure-giving, mind-expanding expression of America in the 20th century, the legacy of a formerly enslaved people that has conquered the world; as an art with its own imperatives, an art that has withstood the test of time and produced a large body of classic work that can withstand not only scrupulous judgment but formal interpretation; an art that continues to produce an extraordinarily high quality of music—then we have not only the right but the obligation to demand support from the public and private sectors.

That jazz has proved itself in the crucible of time is clear from a study of its history, and from present-day responses to works from every stage of its development. When I was in school, a music department chairman told me scornfully, "We'll see if Ellington holds up as well as Stravinsky." Sixty years after *Black and Tan Fantasy*, no one can doubt that Ellington's early miniatures entice us at least as much as Stravinsky's ballets; what's more, late-period Ellington seems to have held up considerably better than late-period Stravinsky, not that it matters one way or the other. When a modern audience encounters stride piano or traditional jazz, it doesn't snicker at what it perceives to be quaintness, as it often does during performances of so-called symphonic jazz or by erstwhile pop stars who embody the nostalgia of a bygone age. Jazz retains the immediacy that once defined the word "classic." Its resilience is beyond dispute, and the primary reason is obvious: the people who pioneer jazz are motivated by the exigencies of art.

One elemental difference between popular and serious art is that the former gives society what it wants while the latter gives it what it needs. If Armstrong embodied the first great leap in jazz history, transfiguring it from a sectarian to an ecumenical phenomenon, Charlie Parker may be said to have embodied the second great leap, introducing modernism with its promise of limitless vistas of emotional and technical range. Parker came along at a time when the country was closing the wounds of fifteen years of economic depression and four years of war. Never was America more vulnerable to the intoxicating qualities of cheap music. The divas of the era sang *I Don't Want to Walk Without You, Accentuate the Positive, Mairzy Doats, Swinging on a Star, Rum and Coca Cola,* and *You'll Never Walk Alone.* Yet Parker and his compatriots in jazz, not all of them members of the bop movement, cut through the sentimentality, the dreamy evasions, the paralyzing fear. They gave us a richly American music, ripe with intensity and vision, that captured the vitality and restlessness of the era. When we hear period songs, we think, "Oh yes, the 40s, how nice." When we hear Parker's *KoKo,* we hear the beating of our own hearts, and even if we know enough musical history to date the performance, neither our emotional response nor our pleasure in the technical achievement is vitiated by the passing decades. Jazz musicians gave us a serious body of music in tune with the true tenor of the times, and therefore capable of speaking to us today. Jazz, not pop and not the academy, told us who we were and where we were headed. We don't find nearly so convincing a record, for example, in the works of Aaron Copland and Roy Harris, those "New York City boys" who, according to historian Samuel Eliot Morison, "applied symphonic methods to jazz and translated this folk art into music."

Still, modernism invariably ruptures the arts community, performers and listeners alike. Sides are drawn. Everyone is forced to choose between past and future, death and life. Those who see the future in the past and vice versa have, of course, chosen life. As John Lewis has noted, jazz was always intended to please and provoke people, to underscore possibilities, not limitations. When Armstrong opted to record *Body and Soul,* he asserted his independence and increased his options. When, thirty years later, Ornette Coleman recorded *Free Jazz,* he was doing the same. Most of us who listen to jazz can appreciate the ties between Armstrong and Coleman, and the bountiful tradition that unites them. Yet not surprisingly, the huge audience raised on jazz as pop did not evolve with the music. The phrase "the jazz community" has become a sour joke, so deep and multifarious are the divisions in that community. The confusion reflected in such divisiveness is magnified by the general misconception concerning jazz's status: is it art or is it pop? Significantly, parallel ruptures between classicism and modernism in the areas of "classical" music, painting, or literature have not resulted in parallel confusion or neglect. In those areas, the academy has found ways to endorse modernism and experimentalism, no matter how wary the public response. Jazz, on the other hand, still resides in a kind of cultural purgatory, as though the jury needed more evidence.

Even so, jazz is now passing through a phase with a potential for great and, in some respects, unexampled aesthetic fulfillment. Never before has jazz been so utterly liberated from the debate over modernism. Jazz is now poised on a plateau where past achievements can be enjoyed without apology, and new ones tasted in the absence of rhetorical subtexts. From the years of Parker's triumphs to the death of John Coltrane, modernism of one sort or another was a rallying point. Musicians in that period were too close to older styles to treat them with dispassion or reverence. They were in the thick of it. Now that jazz has survived the temptations of uninhibited expressionism, the danger in looking back seems to have vanished. All that can gain on you is knowledge. In today's climate, you win points for having done some homework.

Jazz now dazzles itself with its increasing appreciation of its heritage. This isn't the sort of academic appreciation that motivates historians and critics, rather it is an unfettered celebration of options born of the music's first eighty years. This new equanimity encourages musicians to discover classic jazz players for musical reasons—that is, reasons that satisfy the pleasure principle and transcend the tendency to genuflect before designated idols. One reason jazz players have become so self-referential during the past fifteen years is that they find little in the rest of the triangle—the classical and pop angles—to interest them. Armstrong made brilliant use of Arlen and Berlin, and Parker was mesmerized by Stravinsky and Bartók. Since their heirs find far less sustenance in the heirs of Tin Pan Alley and the Franco-Russian academy, they turn to jazz itself for inspiration.

Some commentators are concerned that this generous response to the past is a deathtrap. They imply that if jazz doesn't move ceaselessly forward, like a shark, it will strangle on its own retrospection. Where, they demand, are the great originals? Where is the new Armstrong? the new Ellington? the new Parker? As though genius were something that could be cloned or nurtured like a crop of tomatoes, as if the presence of genius were the only measure by which we might evaluate the health and value of an art. Remembering that other traditions have been able to endure the deaths of Homer, Dante, Michelangelo, Bach, and Shakespeare, we need to give jazz the benefit of the doubt as well. Before allowing jazz to go gentle into that good night, abetted by those all-too-willing pallbearers—commercial indifference, Europhile insecurity, and racial condescension—we must take stock of this miracle music, properly inventory its accomplishments, and wage battle.

Is jazz on the ropes? Not at all. True, most of its guiding lights are gone and its audience is savagely narrowed. The fault, however, lies not in the music. Jazz is presently in the process of consolidating itself to a degree not seen since those early days, when Armstrong learned he could reach more people by putting his stamp on diverse material. I am not suggesting that jazz may enter another cycle of mass popularity; jazz will never (and probably should never) be a pop music again. Nor am I suggesting that the answer lies in facile fusions that bring jazz down to the level of undemanding formulas. But neither should jazz be a lean and hungry cult. After a mere eighty years, during which it has passed through the stages of a folk music, a popular dance music, and an esoteric art music, jazz is now enjoying a balanced reappraisal of its previous stages. Jazz today is not unlike the magical Aleph in the story by Jorge Luis Borges. "An Aleph," Borges wrote, "is one of the points in space that contain all other points." As a musical Aleph, jazz remains intimate with the blues, unembarrassed by pop, unintimidated by the classics of Europe or America, and ready to test itself in areas as discrete as written repertory and free improvisation.

Yet something is terribly amiss. You can't divorce art from the society that produces it, and this society has done its best to divorce itself from jazz. Those who play it or write about it or present it or simply listen to it are so accustomed to slights and inequities that we allow our outrage to be muted. As a community of music lovers, we find ourselves in the position of beggars asking for peanuts and then rejoicing when we get them. Compare the life jazz leads in the United States with the lives of all the other arts. In the century since Emerson called for an American aesthetic, we have learned to take the arts and our role in them seriously. In the century since the performing arts were caged in the rituals of minstrelsy, we have built supermarket arts complexes and produced a mammoth export and import business. We give our artists prizes, chairs, and grants, as well as the other perquisites of a fame-crazy society, from gossipy cover stories to the vacant smiles and handshakes of politicians and movie stars (consider the Kennedy Center Honors). What the marketplace cannot support, the state and the academy help subsidize. Such at least is the case with those arts that are dominated by whites or are heir to the educated European tradition—which, not so incidentally, is the current definition of "classical music": the *American Heritage Dictionary* designates as classical "any music in the educated European tradition, as distinguished from popular or folk music."

How astonishing that the art most neglected by our unofficial ministries of culture, not to mention private enterprise, is one in which American dominance is absolute and unrivaled. In dance, literature, cinema, theater, we are a rich culture among many rich cultures. In music we rule decisively. Even a European phenomenon such as the Beatles is measured, in part, by its relation to African-American precedents. Trap drums and ching-a-ching-ching are ours. The twelve-bar blues, a more durable and influential contemporary form than the twelve-tone row, was developed in the American South. The modern song was perfected on the lower East Side of New York. New instrumental techniques were forged in American communities—chiefly black communities—from coast to coast. Yet jazz is the one area where societal support is most wanting.

The *New Grove Dictionary of Music and Musicians* devotes three times the space to Milhaud as to Ellington; many widely consulted musical encyclopedias lump all jazz artists in a single entry. The principal music critic on every important newspaper in the United States reviews music in the educated European tradition, but isn't obliged to have a working knowledge of jazz—a statistic I find less bothersome than the fact that most of us take it for granted.

During the time required to prepare these comments, I've noted the following indications of jazz's invisibility in its native land. President Reagan recently presented the National Medal of Arts to twelve recipients for the second time, and no representatives of jazz were included. (Teddy Wilson would have been an especially appropriate choice, since everyone knew he was ailing.) The *New York Times* declined to publish obituaries of Jimmy Lyon or Hank Mobley. *The New Criterion* devoted an issue to the state of the arts in New York City, encompassing no less than eighteen areas, without any mention of jazz. The National Jazz Orchestra of France issued a booklet celebrating its government's agreement to meet an annual budget of $1 million; that same week, several American mega-corporations refused any support of the American Jazz Orchestra because, in the words of one vice president, "rock is the future." The French orchestra then proceeded to offer John Lewis, the musical director of the American Jazz Orchestra, a sizable salary to move to Paris as a consultant to that institution. None of this is surprising if you consider the tradition of indifference bordering on contempt with which the arts establishment has long regarded jazz.

One might well ask if America's cultural mandarins think jazz music *is* music. The *New York Times* is ambivalent; not only does it conflate pop and jazz as a single item in its weekday issues, but it maintains an editorial policy in its Sunday Arts and Leisure section that enforces the segregation of jazz-related articles from the Music page. *Time* no longer covers jazz at all; most magazines don't. In 1943 the committee that awards the Pulitzer Prize added a music award that embodied a gentlemen's agreement: eligible works must convey the American spirit, but they must be composed in the educated European tradition. Forty-three years later, the Pulitzer still refuses to acknowledge jazz. Major recording companies no longer feel obliged to record jazz, though they do so from time to time as a relatively cheap means of bolstering slack catalogs. If jazz had the clout of what is perceived as art music in America, recording labels would feel the same pressure to document it as they are to record major symphony orchestras. But given the widespread assumption that jazz is pop—albeit pop that, curiously enough, isn't very popular—they can discharge that responsibility on the grounds that jazz is a specialist interest, better handled by specialty companies. After all, there are no significant prizes or honors for jazz artists in the United States. None. Jazz artists do not get elected to the American Academy of Arts and Letters.

What is most at stake for the young jazz musician is not the potential for being heard or for earning a decent living. What is most at stake are the rudiments of hope. Consider the prognosis from a critic's perspective. If an established literary, film, rock, or classical music critic publishes a long, cogently argued article about a new artist or work in a respectable publication, it will be read not only by his or her colleagues, but by editors, columnists, and publishers outside the field. Whether the subject is Don DeLillo the novelist, Meryl Streep the actress, Prince the rock star, or Yo-Yo Ma the cellist, the artist will enter the mainstream of news coverage, the grapevine of artistic endeavor. All artists abide by the hope that they will at least receive learned appreciation. Yet if every critic at this Wingspread conference were to publish an eloquent article in as many periodicals, in the space of a month, about a particular jazz musician, that musician still wouldn't get signed by Columbia, interviewed on "Live at Five," visited by *People* magazine, or discussed in the *New York Review.* Jazz commentary rarely penetrates the outside world.

I don't believe that the state owes its artists a living. I do believe the state owes its arts a hearing. To support European music, we have the world's most elaborate network of symphony orchestras, chamber ensembles, and an honorable tradition of private and public philanthropy. Jazz is at the stage in its evolution when it must *demand* its fair share. Jazz needs more than parades and flag waving, more than an Ellington stamp or an Armstrong statue, although I am thrilled by those gestures—they are community victories. Monuments honor the dead, and jazz is radiantly alive. Every generation produces another ambitious, gifted slew of players—more than can find work. Jazz needs libraries to house musical scores, orchestras to perform those scores, halls to house the orchestras, and recording labels to document them. It needs scholars and historians; producers, publicists, and managers; and representation in the media, serious journals, and commercial radio. Where are jazz's MBAs, full of yuppie optimism, ready to apply sacred and profane marketing techniques to the promotion of this national resource? Why don't business and government leaders feel as much concern for the preservation of jazz as they do for Italian opera or the Chrysler company?

Nearly seventy years ago, Ernest Ansermet heard the young Sidney Bechet and was reminded of "those men of the 17th and 18th centuries who... mark, not the starting point, but the first milestone" of an art. As we approach the 21st century, it should be obvious that the preservation of jazz's future is inseparable from the preservation of jazz's past, and that both may depend on the present-day recognition of jazz as a cultural landmark that has been grievously underestimated, at least in its native country, for virtually all its life.

The Evolution of Jazz

I have no real quarrel with the observations of my learned friend and colleague, nor with his agenda—and certainly not with that portion of it that asks for greater recognition of the music. Yet it might be useful to approach the subject from a slightly different angle.

While I agree that jazz today finds itself in the postmodern stage, I'm not so sure that the resultant music is best described as neoclassicism. I prefer to think in terms of eclecticism, which the dictionary defines as "selected from various sources and systems according to taste or opinion." That seems closer to the mark than neoclassic, which suggests that the jazz of the 1980s reflects a coherent application of systems and principles accepted as authoritative.

No matter how one approaches it semantically, there can be no doubt that jazz today is much more aware of—and more likely to refer itself to—the "tradition" than ever before, or at least since the advent of jazz modernism. This was an inevitable development. For some four decades, in an astonishing and often more than a little bewildering outpouring of creative energy, jazz underwent rapid and often radical change. This change was dominated by a handful of extraordinary creators and inventors whose originality was strong enough to leave an indelible imprint on the language of jazz. No doubt some learned musicologist (and jazz now has at its service a growing number of these) could, by means of Schenkerian analysis, parse any representative solo by a contemporary jazz improviser who speaks the language fluently, and identify licks and phrases stemming from Armstrong, Young, Parker, and Coltrane for certain—if not also from Hawkins, Gillespie, Tatum, Davis, and Coleman.

But these major shapers of the jazz language all made their impact a generation or more ago, and no figure of comparative magnitude has emerged since then. It's useless to ask whether this is good or bad; suffice it to say that few if any art forms of our time (perhaps with the exception of film, that other prototypically 20th-century mode of artistic expression) can boast of such a list, to which, in the realm of composition and arranging at the very least, the name of Duke Ellington must be added. After such a magnificent outpouring (unprecedented since the Renaissance, said Virgil Thomson, and before the advent of bop at that) of the creative spirit, there almost *had* to come a time to take stock of and digest all the things that had happened so swiftly.

Yet it is also clear, if we look at the other arts, that ours is not a time of significant innovation—to say the least. No new Picasso, Proust, Schoenberg, O'Neill, Frost, or Eisenstein looms on the horizon. We of the jazz world might well take pride in the fact that, excepting a very brief period, our house has largely been free of the unseemly antics or sterile exercises that now pass for art in other realms.

And that is why I part company with Gary Giddins when he suggests that we turn to the academy for sustenance and subsidy. Let us rather rejoice that we have no jazz academy to dictate or suggest directions and fads, and that the state has kept its distance (in this of all centuries, we should know that even a seemingly benevolent state can quickly change its spots). I would rather take chances in the marketplace, as fickle and reprehensible as it might be. It is an option the other arts rightly envy us, and the reason for its existence bears examination.

It may be, as Giddins claims, that jazz has "developed from a functional music (fulfilling the needs of its audience) to a modernist art (which by definition rejects the conventions and expectations of its audience) to various postmodernist movements that reject the expectations not only of the bourgeoisie, but of musicians and critics as well," but I hope not—at least not decisively and irretrievably. The triumph and great strength of jazz, after all, is precisely that it cut through the artificial dichotomy between "serious" and "popular" art that was the creation and legacy of 19th-century European bourgeois culture. Because it originated and developed outside the context of such artificial divisions, jazz was able to reaffirm that the ancient wellsprings of art had not run dry; it was not until it was discovered by the intellectuals and ate of the tree of knowledge, so to speak, that jazz became self-consciously "artistic" and traded its birthright for the mess of pottage from which the other arts had already acquired chronic indigestibility.

I'm not suggesting that the great artists of what Giddins calls jazz's "infancy" (it seems more like its first maturity to me) were "primitives" who had no conscious awareness of what their art and craft were about. Far from it. But they had an audience that looked to them for certain things, and indeed looked *up* to them when they were able to supply these things in such an extraordinary manner, and with such extraordinary style. At first, that audience shared their aspirations and concerns—indeed, it can be said that in their art, these musicians expressed and gave form to the deepest feelings of that audience. Louis Armstrong, whose name and achievement Giddins so frequently invokes, was not, I would suggest, "haunted" by the art-versus-entertainment barbs thrown at him—at most, he was irked. He always had his audience, and its reaction to him was all that mattered. By the latter part of his illustrious career, that audience had grown and changed from a communal to a global one, but he still knew how to make it feel good about itself and about his music.

In his different yet intrinsically related way, Ellington also knew how to accomplish such miracles, and while it is less frequently mentioned today, he too was accused of compromising his art. (Such accusations almost always came from those who had appointed themselves guardians of jazz purity, though their own hands seldom were clean.) Ellington also was able to take such criticism in his stride, but because he moved in more sophisticated circles, he was more vulnerable than Armstrong. Thus, he was genuinely hurt when the Norwegian radio (state-controlled then, like all European broadcasting systems) banned the recording of his delightful (and certainly not disrespectful) interpretation of Grieg's *Peer Gynt* suites. I tried to tell him that Norway was a provincial country and Grieg its only claim to international musical fame, but to no avail. The image he had of Europe as a place of superior cultural values had been damaged.

A quick aside: The whole matter of Europe's supposedly greater appreciation of jazz is a complex and dubious one. On the one hand, it is true that European intellectuals were quicker to realize the significance of jazz than most of their American counterparts, and that some of the earliest perceptive aesthetic commentary on jazz came from European pens. On the other hand, appreciation of jazz was much more widespread among culturally aware Americans than the history books would lead one to believe, even in the 1920s. On the one hand, the relative absence of racism in the pre- and post-Nazi eras made Europe more receptive to and respectful of black artists. On the other, much European jazz commentary, well into the 40s, is embarrassingly patronizing and smug in this regard, sometimes shockingly so to those who harbor illusions. Most significant, American audiences, notably those with a close communal connection to the music, were far more knowledgeable. Take it from one who had the misfortune of being born and raised in Europe at that particular time—and look out for Japan!

The point I am trying to make is this: The astonishing birth and rapid growth of jazz were due to the environment that nurtured it, and that environment was *not* the concert hall. The amazing proliferation of venues where jazz was played—for dancers, for entertainment, and for the pleasure of the musicians themselves—in places like Harlem, Chicago, Kansas City, and dozens of smaller cities and towns throughout this land—made it possible for a generation or two of musicians to hone their skills to the point of perfection. It was inevitable that some of them—the young ones—would reach a stage when they were no longer satisfied to play in any way other than what suited them; that was the stage when jazz became a music exclusively for listening, and when its ties to the community began to wither—not overnight, but gradually.

Something else developed, however: an audience of jazz listeners. The germ of this audience had been there almost from the start, and it solidified in the little clubs on 52nd Street and their counterparts. In Europe it had its start with the "rhythm clubs," mainly made up of record collectors, and these also were formed in the United States. From them sprang the first discographers and historians, and the initial codification of systematized knowledge about jazz. Their efforts soon reflected themselves in the various publications aimed first and foremost at working musicians in the rapidly growing swing band field, whose readership was quickly supplemented by fans. For a while, divergent tastes coexisted in relative peace. The great schism came in the wake of two nearly simultaneous events: the advent of bebop and the rediscovery of traditional jazz.

Though one of these events was musically much more significant than the other, both had vociferous representation in the jazz press, and much mischief was provoked. Underneath the often silly verbiage, however, lay a genuine generational conflict that also involved the representatives of the mature swing style, often overlooked in the debates between progressivists and "moldy figs." The decline of the big bands, largely caused by extramusical factors, was blamed by some musicians on the modernists, both for the nature of their music and for what was perceived, rightly or wrongly, as their abrasive attitude toward the audience and other new behavioral aspects. As with so much in our society, the bottom line was economics.

It was at this juncture that the division within the audience for jazz became most pointed, and the wounds healed slowly. Fences were mended in the 50s, but subsequently new and even more radical developments, in music and in society, again caused splits. Ironically, it was at this time that the term "the jazz community" first was coined, and attempts made to organize. These efforts first came from the musicians themselves—that is to say, from those whose awareness was most acute of the growing alienation between the environment that once had nourished the music and its current practitioners. A number of organizations were formed on idealistic principles; none survived for long in the early years, but later some viable ones emerged. (There will be no listing here, since the inevitable omissions would surely cause aggravation.) These organizations have done much good, and at various times there have been attempts to consolidate communal or regional efforts on a nationwide basis.

I cannot agree that the jazz audience today is "savagely narrowed." On the contrary, it seems to me that it is growing once again, and more important, that it is less fragmented and contentious than before. In this sense, I can agree that we are in a time of great potential promise, but only if we seize the day.

If we indeed have reached a stage in the development of jazz when all manner of styles and approaches are perceived as having the right to exist (which does not require complete agreement about their specific significance), we should also be able to see that jazz has survived because it has more options than other kinds of "serious" music. That it belongs in the concert hall has been a given for almost fifty years, but this does not mean that we have to jettison the clubs— though we should improve the conditions for working (and listening) in them. They provide a link to the past, and a way of preserving the direct and intimate contact between performer and audience that has always been a touchstone of jazz, and also the one venue where musical experimentation and consolidation can take place in a manner impossible on a concert or festival stage. In fact, it would be most useful for repertory orchestras to put in some time in clubs prior to giving concerts, both for artistic and economic reasons.

The relationship between jazz and social dancing has been far more important than almost any commentator except Albert Murray seems to understand. The restoration of this link, which now exists only for a handful of big bands, and on those unmentionable "club dates" that still help to sustain a large number of musicians (even some with fairly established "names"), may prove difficult, but would be worth the effort and certain to attract new audiences.

Even more urgently needed is the restoration of the jam session. On the rather rare occasions when the venerable practice of "sitting in" still occurs, the results are as salutary to musicians as to audiences, but it is primarily for the sake of the former that jamming should be revived. Too many musicians, regardless of stylistic or generational identity, perform within needlessly restricting artistic parameters. The stimulation of contact between generations, once so important to the music, now only seems to take place at stage-managed festival events or within the special restrictions of repertory ensembles; even then, the results are always positive. The initiative will have to come from the musicians themselves, in the absence of resourceful and dedicated session producers such as Milt Gabler, Harry Lim, and the young Norman Granz, who made them work in the past. Benefits and funerals should not be the sole events that bring musicians together to play informally and exchange ideas. (The closest we come these days are the "jazz parties" and jazz cruises, but only the well-to-do can afford to attend these.)

In order to jam, of course, musicians need a common language. There was a time, not so long ago, when the basic common language of jazz seemed in danger of extinction. Once again, however, almost everyone who aspires to the title of jazz musician at least seems able to handle blues or *I Got Rhythm* changes. Still, one can't be so sure about the songs known as "standards," even among players who invoke the jazz heritage. Yet it seems to me that the ability to put yourself into a familiar old song (or a good new one, if any are around) and recast it in your own image, supported by others who speak a shared musical tongue, remains the magic formula for keeping the jazz tradition alive, and the true test of originality and invention.

Does it go without saying that the results should also swing? That may be a loaded question. The element of swing remains one of the key discoveries of jazz, and one that isn't easy to appropriate. Yet younger musicians have been surprisingly willing to trade it in, for much less striking "innovations."

All that is to say that we can't expect outsiders to honor the jazz tradition if we fail to do so ourselves—and we have often failed in the past. I'm not so sure America's cultural mandarins routinely show contempt for jazz. The *New York Times* may fail from time to time, but it provides more regular coverage of jazz than any other newspaper in the world, and if that coverage is not always ideal—well, what newspaper coverage of any aspect of culture ever was? If *Time* no longer covers jazz, that may be lucky for us. The *New Yorker* has covered it for about thirty years, and the *Village Voice* has Giddins and Stanley Crouch. As the keeper of a jazz archive that attempts to collect and preserve all writing on the subject, I see a tremendous amount of coverage. It's not always, or even often, very well informed, but we cannot honestly claim that jazz is ignored by the print media.

Even television is not a wasteland, though opportunities are often bungled. And the jazz video market is growing apace. As for recordings, while it is true that the major companies in this country seldom discharge their obligation to make the past accessible to the present, and certainly often fail to make the best of the present available at all, the enormous proliferation of jazz recordings worldwide is more than even professional listeners can keep up with. I doubt that any other form of non-pop music is better represented, quantitatively speaking. Adequate distribution and sufficient exposure are other matters, but these will be addressed elsewhere. And since we always seem so intent upon comparing ourselves unfavorably with classical music, let it be noted that the New York Philharmonic has been without a recording contract for several years, and that the Metropolitan Opera has had to discontinue, after forty years, its national touring program. Of course jazz needs more support and respect, but we do have gifted performers *and* an audience, and both are enviable life-supports. That is not to say we shouldn't demand our just share of the cultural funding pie—which our present elected leaders seem eager to eliminate!

The teaching of jazz is another subject to be addressed elsewhere. But I must say one thing, not about formal jazz (or music) education, but about something much more basic: It is scandalous that not one American history textbook, on any level, that I know of, has anything to tell our children about the greatest and most original music this country has created, and about the creators of that music. Are they taught that Louis Armstrong and Duke Ellington are two of the greatest figures of this century? That black Americans created a music that has conquered the world, and from which all the musics the children do know have sprung? And do they hear that music? This is something we must address, with help from our friends in the political sector. *That* is fundamental.

There has never been any doubt in my mind that jazz will survive as long as people have the desire to make music. Perhaps, at this particular juncture in its history, we will finally manage to bring together all the many people from all walks of life who love jazz, and bring pressure to bear to make its survival a bit easier and more rewarding. It surely is about time!

Jazz Criticism and Its Effect on the Art Form

Criticism, ideally, should be analysis, but also identification and *use,* based upon a work, its creator's intent and values, and their relationship to the real world. How exemplary the work is of this intent and values is what we are analyzing, and what this means practically. What is key is that the critic actually understand what the work intends, that is, what it means to mean as well as how close it comes to meaning it.

The critic should attempt to uncover the reality of the work, what it actually is and does, illuminating the creator and his conception together as part of a material world. But no analysis is valuable without the critic's being at least familiar with the premises and presumptions of the work and its creator, as well as the real-life context it issues from.

Given the specific aggregate of values and philosophy that is one dimension of both the form and the content of a work, we must know what the work and the artist are saying and their real-life significance, as well as the "grammar" and record-keeping aspect of an art—that is, identification of genre, artistic school, and influences, though even these categorizations are useful in fully explicating any important work and artist.

What *Blues People* raised to a certain extent was the significance of "criticism" issuing from writers and institutions whose values and aesthetic were antithetical to the values and aesthetic of the artists themselves, as well as to the essentially black mass audience for whom the works were created. Basically the contrasts of philosophy, values, and aesthetic would be in opposition, as slave versus slave master.

The situation is so ironic as to elicit continuous, at times hysterical, laughter. First "they" steal us from our homelands, make us slaves, make generations of the African American people, even now, in closer intimacy with hourly tragedy than almost anyone in North America. Now they want to "judge" our art. But to the slave master, the art of the slaves is first of all *slave "art."* What is even displayed of it, the slave master "understands," is permitted with his *tolerance.* Since blacks still have no institutions, albeit the church, the beggar or white man's burden still hangs about the African American people, making our economic and political weaknesses as glaring as they are crippling. This is the question Du Bois raised in *The Souls of Black Folk:* What is it like to see yourself through the eyes of those who despise you? This is the source of black petit bourgeois self-hatred and defeat, a syndrome or "double consciousness," which Du Bois baits with: How to be black and American?

One expression of the conglomerate of oppression-created relationships (historically moving from the slave-holding society to its more camouflaged contemporary continuation) is the assumption of the inferiority of everything African and black. Indeed western capitalism's domination of the world was fueled *fundamentally* by African slavery and the conquest of India. Black exploitation is one of the most glaring aspects of world capitalism.

In the earliest years of black presence in the New World, black art was initially (after the conquest) a *threat.* It could fuel and communicate rebellion. The drum was banned, which should draw attention to its *political* nature. Substitution for the drum brought the steel band in the West Indies, but it also deepened and made even more profound the slaves' vocal music. The rhythmic sophistication of the African was forced into vocal expression that was highly sophisticated from its beginnings, if we are to judge from recordings of the Babenzele pygmies, as well as Leon Thomas's adaptation of their "hocketing" or yodeling style. A percussive style was brought to any instrument blacks played—fiddle, jawbone, broom, body, feet, sticks, and later to horns, even piano, though by that time the drum was allowed. But to this day, as Max Roach says, "drums are the niggers of the orchestra."

Just as black persons were systematically humiliated so that they would submit more easily to chattel slavery, so the slave empire's history writers, philosophers, critics, academics, and institutions "inferiorized" African culture. In the chronicle-sized poem of many songs I am writing about African American history called *Why's/Wise*, the griot tells us in the first poem:

Wise 1
(Nobody Knows the Trouble I Seen)
If you ever find
yourself, some where
lost and surrounded
by enemies
who wont let you
speak in your own language
who destroy your statues
& instruments, who ban
your omm boom ba boom
then you are in trouble
deep trouble
they ban your
omm boom ba boom
you are in deep deep
trouble

humph!
probably take you several hundred years
to get
out!

The much-discussed destruction of African culture was a basic re-
quirement for reducing the slaves to unconscious instruments of gain.
The slave was, himself, a part of the means of production—a tool.

The rewriting of history which Du Bois, the father of black studies,
pointed out was repeated throughout the slave society's superstructure, to justify and legitimize slavery. Duke Ellington cannot be
allowed to be the world-class creator that he is, because if Duke is
Duke or Zora Neale is Zora Neale, what does that do to white
supremacy as an idea? If the slave society has to deal with the
historical reality and facts of the African people—the first humans,
the harnessers of fire, the creators of language, song, dance, clothing,
and art itself—then how does it explain why they are now clamped
in chains?

The main institutions of jazz criticism are like any of the more basic
American institutions in relationship to the African American people:
they are white supremacist, fundamentally exploitative, and self-
serving. Earlier, these critical institutions simply dismissed African
culture as savage, or later as nonexistent, as the alien African became
the more familiar Negro slave. The only "culture" and art a slave had
were, at most, imitative and witless. One has only to read 19th-century
observers and "scholars" such as Krehbiel and Kemble to understand
this attitude.

A relationship based on slavery and repression, like that which
defines U.S. society, is likewise based on the "inferiority" of those
oppressed, materially and philosophically. Ironically, though,
African American culture, art, and even, finally, political utterance is
such a combustible, catalytic substance within the broader American
culture that its transforming, advanced, and radical force (in the
context of its being a slave/oppressed projection in spite of and in
opposition to the dominant culture) must politically be "covered."

Economically, its covering is the identical social act that distinguished slavery. Minstrelsy, for instance, explains a critical economic relationship as well as a social and political one. It is like wearing the skin of a slain beast! The "advance" of American society is seen in the fact that now minstrelsy is "respectable"—it pretends to be real, simply another "style."

Equally masked is the continued and constantly paralleled exploitation of black Americans. The relationship of America to black people generally follows the same fundamental relationship the society has with black art and culture. In the same way that the dominant society, through its economic-political repression and social and cultural chauvinism, crushes black people, so any segment or vector of it has a similar relationship. This includes the "official" criticism of black music, that is, that which is best financed, whether "independent," university, or other powerful institution. Media, government, and corporate bodies are, in their objective effect, parallel to the main focus of the superstructure.

African culture and European and colonial Euro-American culture were quite different traditions, even before the enforced "intimacy" of the slave trade. In music, for instance, the rhythmic sophistication of the African culture can be contrasted to the harmonically developed European musical aesthetic.

The historically consistent aesthetic of Africa and African American music, Du Bois pointed out, was linked directly to the oldest religion, the "faith of our fathers." Music itself was indispensable to the worship, likewise to the central role of the priest. The call-and-response form found in most black music represents a dialogue between the shepherd and his flock, and the frenzy (spirit possession) that accompanied these is a basic fabric of spirit worship itself.

"The spirit will not descend without song," the Africans said. The frenzy, what we called "gettin' happy" in the Baptist Church, is the method of communication with and possession by the spirit. This spirit possession is the highest religious expression—becoming animated by the divinity as life force.

This is the religious content, its forms existing to obtain or display this content: screams, shouts, moans, stomps, tearing the air wildly, staring pop-eyed into space, quivering like a cosmic gong. These are forms of God: world into us as itself, and as ourselves in it of it unconsciously superconscious of all of it (as or against the "not it").

Black music is meant anthrophilosophically, historically, to bring worshipers into unity with the super-being (*all*-being), with the Holy Spirit. "He went Out!" we say, in 1986. This is the African cultural thrust—seen in specific reference to art, philosophy, religion, and society as an aesthetic, or a basic and abiding part of that aesthetic. The other world-connecting aspects of that aesthetic are the exact condition of the human bearers of this aesthetic, and how an aesthetic is one expression of a worldview: subjective, yet reflective of objective political and economic existence.

Black culture has been a slave of racist America. Black art has been kept in chains. The critical establishment erected in the name of and on the backs of black music is its abusive overseer. The commercial and corporate wealth reaped by the exploitation of black culture is inestimable. Michael Jackson saved Columbia Records' popular music division, before he was nearly banished for consorting with black people (his family) in the act of trying to make $100 million and wanting to celebrate that *Victory* with the infamous nigger promoter of evil bloody boxing, Don King.

The slave versus slave-master society still exists, as it must, today. The destruction of Stax records, the co-optation and dilution of Motown, the reduction of many small black recording and production companies to "independent" producers for the big houses are all historically classic. Democracy is seen as *competition* in a society where everything is a commodity.

Barbra Streisand is no Aretha Franklin (no one else is either). Cyndi Lauper cannot be either—ask Patti LaBelle. But it is Streisand (or Dinah Shore) who makes the millions, has the television or movie career. The "cover" was a blind to suck blood; Dracula in "black face," so no one is wise.

But times change. Debussy, Ravel, Ansermet, Brecht, Stravinsky, Panassie, Berendt, Hodeir, Copland, Ives, Gershwin, European and white American jazz players, the American theater, the Lost Generation, Langston Hughes, the Harlem Renaissance, Vachel Lindsay, the Beat Generation, the New York school, the Black Mountain school, Picasso, Matisse, German expressionism, Jackson Pollock, abstract expression, Merce Cunningham, George Balanchine, Leonard Bernstein—all these progressive sectors of America and Europe saw to some of that explanation in the mainstream when it was "avant." The primary creators of the music, largely African American, saw to the expression, the "telling of the story," while national and international social, economic, and political conditions set the real-life pressures and transformations.

The largely white critical establishment living off black music shapes less sophisticated tastes. It can create "stars," geniuses, fortunes, and fiction. It can also stop them. Yet historically, the American, essentially white-owned, critical establishment has been the most overtly racist in the world. The national oppression-based superstructure made it more difficult to judge black music as an independent, self-determining expression.

The blues is what black people are as music. It is what black life is, too. The critical establishment masks its oppressive relationship to black music and musicians with formalism and distorted history. Formalism normally stresses form over content. The formalism of the jazz critical establishment celebrates form as content and as formal "invention." Craft and structure are exalted, but "objectionable" content is denigrated as having flaws in technique.

Nevertheless, the "story," the content of black music, tells us of black life in America. It's all in there. The music itself serves as definer and resister to the "world of trouble" America has been for the African American nation. It exists as proof of the lie of the slave society, the hypocrisy of American "civilization." It accuses and denounces and exposes as consistently as it loves and laughs. And it does this as part of the "highest" art this society has produced.

Discuss Langston Hughes and William Carlos Williams seriously, or Ellington and Stravinsky, and you will begin to understand. But black culture is radical within the context of the slavery-based and white-supremacy-rooted U.S. society; as a reflection of the African American people, it is part of the struggle for democracy and self-determination. The most advanced projections of that culture carry that life, that focus, that history in varying degrees of consciousness. Amilcar Cabral said "the culture of the people is the repository of resistance" to national oppression. African American art is the griot's tale of the nation's travail. From the oldest work songs in African languages to the new new music. From gutbucket to avant gutbucket.

The resistance, in turn, of the racist society to the black struggle for democracy has been world-advertised. The American critical establishment first resisted the idea that African Americans were human beings who could even produce art. Although slavery ended, white supremacy was not suppressed, as the destruction of Reconstruction and the emergence of the "separate but equal" doctrine readily attest. The upsurge of black writers on jazz in the 1960s was a reflection of the black masses' simultaneous cry for self-determination (at its most practical, beginning with self-definition).

Objectively as well, the official, mostly white critical establishment is linked to powerful corporate and commercial interests upon which it depends for financial support, whether through advertising, consultancies, foundation grants, corporate gifts, and so on. For this reason the commercial dilutions of jazz usually transform competent white players into "stars," "geniuses," and "innovators," while deprecating the black innovators. It's obvious that the critical establishment, linked directly to the corporate-commercial establishment, can make millionaires of white players, while the actual black initiators and innovators of the style (whom the corporate and critically supported players are replicating) might literally starve to death.

It is the ideological and cultural nature of the music business's corporate owners to oppose any "radicalism" generally, and to water such expression down for commercial exploitation, regardless of the nationality. (It is "eaten.") For example, there is no auto industry—

they make cars to make money. Publishing deals seek books that will make profit, with certain clear "ideological" guidelines. "Art" in general is viewed as a snide joke, an obstruction to profit-taking. Everything is literally reduced to filthy lucre, i.e., *shit*.

Decaying capitalism reduces all of its own institutions to money worship, which in turn reduces human transformational experiences to the passage of commodities and the owing and collecting of money. Our capitalist leaders would reduce the entire world to a large bank with automatic, twenty-four-hour pay-and-grab machines installed in our homes, cars, and clothes.

Such is the basis of the establishment's "aesthetic" and critical standards. The common assumption that European music is superior to African music reflects the philosophy and aesthetic values of slavery and fascism. This view—an expression of white supremacy—is quite respectable in the United States, up to the highest-ranked racists in the society (academic, cultural, political, and artistic).

For the black artist, this continuing national oppression of his community produces a super-exploitation. Not even the ordinary "bourgeois democracy" that exists for working-class whites exists for the black masses. For instance, 30 million African Americans lack a single U.S. senator to "represent" them. In the music business, super-exploitation means hit songs bought for a few pennies, while the corporations make millions. It means heavy-thumbed promoters and agents ripping off black musicians with impunity, as part of the social and economic tradition of white supremacy.

Duke Ellington had to list exploiting producers as co-composers in order to get his music distributed. It's no wonder that Duke, Count, Billie, Trane, Monk, Papa Joe, Philly Joe, Mary Lou Williams, and Louie are already dead, while their promoters, producers, and agents—most around the same age—are alive, well-off, and still making money off the dead folks' work!

Since the 50s and the emergence of rock and roll, there have been even more jazz- and blues-influenced white musicians and singers who could be celebrated, promoted, and made rich: "The King of Jazz," "The King of Swing," "The Best Rock and Roll Band in the

World." Now they are even calling Bette Midler "The Divine," and Bruce Springsteen "The Boss." There have been movies about Janis Joplin, Glenn Miller, Benny Goodman, Bix Beiderbecke, Red Nichols, and Helen Morgan—just like we have films about Graziano and LaMotta, but none about Sugar Ray. But the "covers" and segregation did not necessitate anything more from the mainstream critical establishment and corporate music-business owners than patronizing chauvinism toward the black sources.

The social progress of black people and the more objective analyses of European and non-American critics, however, raised the music to a point of visibility in the U.S. mainstream that it had never directly had before. Since the Harlem Renaissance, its accompanying "Jazz Age," and the arrival of blues and related black musics into the big cities of the United States, black music and its influence have been more visible. This visibility and international praise for and valorization of the music, plus its deepening influence on U.S. society (especially white youth), have made it necessary not only to cover black musicians and their hits; since Presley, it has been apparent that the critical establishment and the corporate owners now want to project whites as the real innovators and significant stylists of the music. (I discussed this in "The Great Music Robbery," in *The Music: Reflections on Jazz and Blues*, New York: William Morrow & Co., 1987.)

Chauvinist garbage like Len Lyons's *Great Jazz Pianists* excludes Duke, Monk, Tatum, Waller, Bud, Willie the Lion, and James P. Johnson! It includes Joe Zawinul, Jimmy Rowles, Keith Jarrett, Paul Bley, Dave Brubeck, Marian McPartland, George Shearing, Steve Kuhn, Chick Corea, and Ran Blake! The same author's *100 Greatest Jazz Records* is filled with similar twisted racism, there being more of those "greatest" from Corea and Zawinul than Bud Powell. The Reagan-led rightward motion of society is clearly duplicated by the steady flow of chauvinist, reactionary scribbling passing as commentary or analysis of the music. Consider, for example, Jack Chambers's incredibly racist books on Miles Davis, one of the main themes of which is that Miles played his best when he played with white musicians! Or Lincoln Collier, whose various writings give off a distinct aroma of rotting mint julep.

The older, more outrightly racist denunciation of the music has been succeeded by an equally racist attempt to pirate it. Every major writing job on African American music is held by whites. Most institutions that deal with it are white-dominated. As an entity, the critical institutions related to black music should at best be secondary and modified adjuncts to an African American and progressive critical institutional process.

Economic development, at one point, is an expression of conscious cultural development. Black music alone, as a developed industrial, commercial, academic, artistic, and professional complex, could have supported millions of African Americans based on performing, editing and writing, scholarship and research, recording, video production, publishing (music and related books and periodicals), audio, technology and electronics, design, maintenance, graphics, management (booking clubs, theaters, and concert halls), legal, manufacturing and packaging, distribution and sales, mail order, and so on. But most of these jobs are held by whites, because of the exploitative and racist structure of U.S. society.

Most individual performers work at laughable wages, though sometimes accompanied by lavish "praise" or even elevation to the status of "legend" or "genius." Such labels attempt to mask the slave economic conditions of these truly great artists. In many cases, though, it has been the very hostility of the critical establishment that has prevented innovative black artists from being respected and celebrated in a *real* way, that is, to make a decent living from their art. *Down Beat*'s attacks on Charlie Parker, Miles Davis, Dizzy Gillespie, and some of the music's great classics when they first appeared could be cited. *Down Beat* re-reviewed the recordings after it *had* to, when Bird, Miles, and Diz began to be recognized as the great creators they are. The first reviews gave no stars, the second, five! Such an about-face demonstrated hindsight and dishonest critical mutation, but neither principles nor intelligent, informed analysis.

The attacks on John Coltrane were infamous. His transcendently beautiful sound was called "ugly." A remarkably gentle person, Trane was constantly described as "angry." I remember one reviewer calling Coltrane's playing "barbaric yawps." (Check the recorded interview with a Scandinavian journalist on the recently released *Miles Davis & John Coltrane in Sweden* [Dragon].) Yet Coltrane was a major innovator and artist. His contributions took black music into another era, literally expanding the perceived range and articulation of the tenor saxophone while reflecting through exact emotional analogy the turbulent period in which he lived.

In this sense the critical establishment, like U.S. society itself, consistently attacks jazz's profoundest advances and innovations, objectively and aggressively opposing and weakening the music's legitimate historical development. The criticism openly attempts to retard the music and make independent development impossible.

But the music, like the people, retains its own independent motion, no matter what the irrelevant abuse of the critical establishment. The styles of black music evolve as open rebellion against the aesthetic (and social) dilution of the previous style perpetrated by the corporate deculturization process. White Dixieland's dilution of New Orleans style was, in one aspect, simply an indication that the most contemporary genre of black music had already changed.

When corporate big bands and their arranged nonswing reached their most devastating stage of dilution, the boppers arrived at Minton's to collectively create a new black musical form, which emerged to refocus on the classic African polyrhythms, the historical profundity of the blues, and the critical importance of improvisation: bebop.

Bebop was "monkey music," "Chinese music," "scandalous," "madness," "crazy," a "con game." One critic even called it "Stalinist"! Yet soon enough, as the style became more familiar and presumably more accessible, the corporations came out with the "West Coast" and "cool" white commercial styles, as a watery ripoff of the real.

Meanwhile, the most advanced stream of African American music had already created an antidote for the commercialism: "hard bop." This style went back to the black church, particularly in its gospel voice (the mating of the spiritual with the blues). "Soul," "funk," and the basic historical spirituality of the African American culture were summoned to reclaim the music from white supremacy and commercial destruction.

A little later, the classic Miles Davis group, Sonny Rollins, John Coltrane, brought and inspired new developments: the so-called "new music" or "avant-garde." These directions were picked up by such younger heads as Ornette Coleman, Cecil Taylor, and Pharaoh Sanders. Yet all these important innovators at different points in the music's history were attacked by the aggressive, chauvinist critical structure. And this abets the social and economic robbery which the class that "prices" art commits.

To write, as Whitney Balliett wrote in the *New Yorker*, that the major women singers were Bessie, Billie, Ella, and Anita O'Day, and that the most influential was primarily Ms. O'Day, is about chauvinism more than music. That is defining the original by the copy. (Where is Sarah Vaughan?)

Robert Palmer of the *New York Times* (a good old Ivy type of good old boy) suggests that pianist Bill Evans was the major stylistic innovator and primary influence on contemporary jazz pianists. In reality, Miles wanted Ahmad Jamal; Evans was one of several pianists who approximated that style. Evans has been given a lot of ink. The white musician who is skilled and plays with a historically important group such as Miles's will receive all the publicity there is. But to say that Evans was the *innovator*, the primary influence on recent jazz musicians, is to reverse Evans's role and to belittle Jamal, not to mention the great and highly influential Red Garland and McCoy Tyner, nor does it take into account Cecil Taylor or the avants. And of Evans's peers, surely Wynton Kelly was one of the swingingest mo' fo's on the set, and Tommy Flanagan could match Evans sensitivity for sensitivity.

Beside the constant and humiliating racism that the critical establishment dispenses, there is also the question of this establishment's
aesthetic. I went into this as far as I could in *Blues People*. There is—and
the white-supremacist foundations of the society make it obvious and
presumed—a marked and sharp aesthetic contradiction between the
creators of the music and the critical establishment erected on its back.
Such aesthetic contrast reflects and confirms a basic philosophical
"distance"—the distance between slave and slave master, between
oppressed and oppressor. There is also the philosophical contradiction between Europe and Africa, which stretches back into the mists
of history. But people who have lived in the same society would
ordinarily have more nearly merged into a new entity combining both
originals. The U.S. melting pot has done this for Europeans here, who
are now almost homogeneously American. The Africans, however,
have not been allowed to "melt." Slavery and segregation saw to that,
while racism and white supremacy see to its continuing.

White supremacy in the United States is not simply philosophy,
but an imposed method of social organization, because it creates an
artificial and tragic social division, maintaining an aesthetic distance
between the African American people and whites. The post-50s rock
phenomenon shows how aesthetic distance is broken down; for example, rock and roll is not "influenced" by rhythm and blues, it *is*
rhythm and blues, appropriated by whites. White supremacy, however, made a wholly "original," wholly "independent" white music
with no connections to its obvious parent, or its brothers and sisters.

The Euro-American aesthetic takes Europe as its star of faith (even
up to and past the Beatles), though "place" identification can be
replaced by the dollar. The performer with the most platinum or the
biggest hit often becomes the "first ancestor" and setter of historic
standards. "Europe" means the culture of the free and white, but there
is also a class significance to this "whiteness," not just a racial question. The economics are basic, but there is a class aesthetic as well, tied
to race because who got the money had to be in a position to get it,
although now such class attitudes are made more ubiquitous by the
advance of technology. Obviously the commercial imitation can even

influence players with potentially something much more original to say.

A class note can be sounded by just an emotional commitment to the tempered scale, the jig or ditty, European song or dance form, academic formalism (form celebrated over content), the softened timbres of well-being as opposed to the desperate screams of those for whom they themselves have said, "Nobody Knows the Trouble I Seen." The use of commercial gimmickry over emotional force. The nonblues blues imitation. The philosophical focus on the socially irrelevant or unimportant, pornography, silliness, devil worship, "out," psychological states, and so on. The life and times of white teenagers' fantasy (as synthesized by adult merchants) and near-real nonbeing.

To be sure, there is genuinely progressive and advanced music created by white musicians. But the society itself demands mediocrity and catatonia from *everybody!* The arrogance and ignorance of America's leaders confirm the common psychological development that defines a common culture. Ronald Reagan, the president of the United States—that is a grimmer condemnation than anything I could more abstractly conceive!

Since whites are, in the main, part of the fabric of decadent U.S. imperialism, they are connected in a more direct and organic way. Blacks, on the other hand, have never been admitted. It is that enforced separation that creates despair but at the same time prevents blacks from fully embracing the decadent commercialism of U.S. society in its last days.

This separation produces the classic tension of an art that is outside and inside the dominant society at the same time. It involves the same tragedy, bitter irony, national consciousness, humor, self-deprecating rage, and human heroics that have provided a line of demarcation between Irish and English literature these many years.

From the black religion of the old country until the present day, passion is not an adjunct but an end, as an instrument of knowledge. The music is *about feeling:* the feeling generated by black life, which is defined by its opposition (contradiction) to the dominant culture. Its most advanced (even its healthiest) existence is in some fashion predicated on resistance. This is what Cabral meant when he said that the culture of the oppressed exists at its most essential as a proof that people have survived and have not been liquidated by imperialism, its cultural aggression and genocide.

The slave's feelings are so important because all else is denied. The slave is property, without history, culture, status, or future. Only his feelings deny this slave existence, in opposition to the slave master's view of the world.

The most dangerous thing about the slave's feelings is that they are the deepest source of living resistance to slavery, whether expressed as words or as music. But if the slave's deepest feeling is anti-slavery, slavery's continuing presence remains the essence of contemporary U.S. social relations. At its deepest consciousness, the black liberation movement remains in sharp conflict with its enemies, even in the arts.

However, as African Americans' level of productive forces (their educational and social development, and the technology they have access to) rises, so too does the possibility of black institutions that can objectively analyze and "measure" black arts from the general aesthetic perspective and common psychological development of African American culture.

Mao Tse-tung wrote that the area of arts criticism is one of intense class struggle. The critical subjugation of the black arts—jazz included—by the racist U.S. critical establishment is just one more aspect of black oppression.

Stanley Crouch, *Respondent*

Jazz Criticism and Its Effect on the Art Form

When I received a copy of the preceding paper, it appeared to have been written in one sitting, its very sloppiness symbolic of the lack of aesthetic seriousness so obvious in its content. In an effort to reduce the artistry of jazz to no more than political pulp, LeRoi Jones* has simplified the complexity of inspiration, invention, adaption, and context to a battlefield on which black victims war against a conspiracy of racist corporate heads and white jazz writers. Clearly, any analysis of Negro American history that ignores racism as an enduring element would be naive. But what Lincoln Kirstein called a "lazy bravado" (to describe what we have now come to expect from tenured Marxist revolutionaries) so dominates Jones's thesis that the grandeur of an internationally influential music has been reduced to either the

---

*Throughout his paper, Stanley Crouch chose to refer to Amiri Baraka by his original name, LeRoi Jones.

cries of the victimized or the anthems of a homemade, far-left square dance. Jones further convolutes his largely hysterical argument by describing jazz as a latter-day variation on possession-oriented African religion, as well as an expressive protest against the conventions of Western art and the economics of capitalism. Only LeRoi Jones could try to strap such a lightweight saddle to the galloping horse of jazz and expect us to miss the fact that all he largely has to offer is a mouthful of dust.

But what we must address here, and what Jones clearly avoids as often as possible, is factual information that will provide us with a better understanding of the art itself and the strengths as well as the shortcomings of jazz criticism. It is quite true that spirit worship and possession were central to the music of the Africans brought into the Western Hemisphere as slaves. It is equally true that the drums were usually suppressed when it was learned that they could send messages. Yet it is also true that in the Northeast during the colonial era, slaves were allowed to celebrate holidays playing drums and performing African dances, as Eileen Southern documents in *The Music of Black Americans*. She also makes it clear that as early as the late 18th century, Negroes were influencing popular dance rhythms with qualities that became universally popular. But those black people who played fiddles during bondage or as free citizens were the result of a social crucible that produced perhaps the most influential synthesis of Western and non-Western ideas since the indelible impact of the Moors on Spanish and southern European cultures. They were a new people—some mixed with European blood, some with that of the American Indian, some with Hispanic tributaries in their family lines. Above all, the raw impositions of slavery ironically liberated them from the tribal enmities and religious conflicts that still bedevil contemporary Africa, allowing for a richly distinctive Negro American sensibility of remarkable national consequence.

What they maintained of their African heritage is far more important to this discussion and to American culture than what they were forbidden to perpetuate, what they lost, or what they forgot. What existed within the ritual confinements of polytheistic African cultures and has been dubbed "an affinity for distortion" was transmogrified into what I call a sense of infinite plasticity. In Africa, this sense of plasticity has been observed in the stretching of necks with rings, the extending of lips with wooden plates, the filing of teeth, the elasticizing of slit earlobes so that they could hold large wooden discs, and so on. The plasticity of stylization in African singing allowed for a scope that included falsetto, whistles, tongue-clicking, shouts, plaintive to joyous slurs, growls, and enormous changes of register, rhythm, timbre, accent, and intensity. That the shifts of meter, tempo, and accent in African drumming reflect this sense of plasticity almost goes without saying, as should any observation about dancing that demands independent coordination of the head, shoulders, arms, trunk, and legs. As any contemporary visual artist knows, African masks are also given to plastic distortion, with their multiple heads, huge eyes, angularity, intricate rhythms, and the near-collision of materials—beads, stone, mud, wood, straw, metal, animal skins, blood.

This disposition, this sense of plasticity or "affinity for distortion," had an impact on professional Negro musicians at the same time that it was functioning in a folk context. As we also learn from Southern's *The Music of Black Americans*, by 1818 the immensely popular Frank Johnson's Colored Band was observed "distorting a simple, and beautiful song, into a reel, a jig, or country dance." In other words, Johnson, who was a resident of Philadelphia, was rhythmically rearranging the familiar in a surprising fashion, setting a precedent for what we would later hear from jazz musicians such as Roy Eldridge, who in 1938 followed the slow rendition of *Body and Soul* with a classic, up-tempo improvisation. Johnson also predicted the popularity of the golden era of Negro jazz bands that played for dances across America. Johnson led marching bands up and down the East Coast, even as far south as Richmond, Virginia, where one planter wrote of his ensemble, "who ever heard better dance music than this?" In 1838, eighty-one years before Ernest Ansermet was stunned by Sidney Bechet's improvisations with Will Marion Cook's Southern Syncopated Orchestra during a European tour in 1919,

Johnson made old England quite merry as he traveled, putting his
Negro American rhythms on listeners and receiving a silver bugle for
his efforts when he played a Buckingham Palace command performance for Queen Victoria.

Between Frank Johnson and the jazz improvisation that was
brought to revolutionary fruition by Louis Armstrong, the folk source
of the Negro spiritual introduced a sense of profound joy and tragedy,
an emotional bloom of maturity that evolved into the bittersweet
power of the blues, that least sentimental of American vocal musics.
Somewhere between the spiritual and the blues arrived ragtime, a
popular dance music that extended the precedents set by Frank
Johnson's Colored Band. As Roger Pryor Dodge observed in *Harpsichords and Jazz Trumpets* in 1934:

> Ragtime, we now perceive, was the rhythmical twist the negro gave to the
> early American dance tune. Here, the different instruments were finding
> their place in the musical pattern and already daring to add their own
> peculiar instrumental qualities. But—suddenly, the whole breadth of
> melodic and harmonic difference between the *folk-tune* stuff Ragtime was
> made out of, and the Chant stuff the racial Blues were made out of, touched
> something very deep in the negro. He found himself going way beyond
> anything he had done so far. For he had now incorporated his own melodic
> Blues within his own syncopated dance rhythms and miraculously created
> a new music—a new music which moved him so emotionally that Jazz
> bands sprang up like mushrooms all around him. The Blues, retrogressed
> hymn, secular spiritual, had fathered itself by way of the clarinet, trumpet,
> trombone, banjo, drums and piano into a rebirth, and christened itself
> JAZZ!

Dodge's writing presented the richest ideas in early jazz criticism
because he heard the art within a serious context, understanding that
improvisation wasn't the incredibly new thing many thought it to be,
pointing out that "If we turn to the musical literature of the 17th and
18th centuries we find that no two artists were supposed to play
identical variations and ornaments on the same piece; on the contrary,
the artist was expected extemporaneously to fill in rests, ornament the

whole notes and rhythmically break up chords. The basic melody, as in Jazz, was considered common property. If the player exactly imitated somebody else or faithfully followed the written composition of another composer, he was a student, not a professional." As a dancer, Dodge wasn't put off by the fact that jazz was performed for a dancing public. Still describing the 17th- and 18th-century European context, he went on to say:

> At that time one listened first, as one does now in Jazz, for the melody, then recognized the variations as such and drew intense enjoyment from the musical talent familiarly inspired. Instead of waiting months for a show piece to be composed and then interpreted (our modern academic procedure), then, in one evening, you could hear a thousand beautiful pieces, as you can now in Jazz. Instead of going to a dance hall to hear Armstrong, in earlier times you might have gone to church and heard Frescobaldi; or danced all night to Haydn's orchestra; or attended a salon and listened to Handel accompany a violinist—with his extemporaneous variations so matter of course; or sneaked in on one of Bach's little evenings at home, when to prove his theory of the well-tempered clavier he would improvise in every key, not a stunt improvisation in the manner of someone else, but preludes and fugues probably vastly superior to his famous notated ones.

Dodge then made a point that is perhaps even more important today than it was half a century ago, given the irrefutably dull ways in which students tend to play the transcriptions learned in most jazz teaching situations:

> Academicians of today can improvise in the styles of various old schools but the result is commonplace, not only because the fact of improvising in a school that is out of date, but because such an urge is precious and weak in itself, limiting the improvisor to forms he has already seen in print. Even in contemporary modern music, the working out is so intellectual that the extempore act does not give the modernist time to concoct anything he himself would consider significant.

I would strongly disagree with the idea that certain jazz schools might now be considered out of date: classic languages have been developed since Dodge's era that can inspire young improvisors to find their own identities, just as developing artists with a variety of schools to choose from within a given idiom have always done, given the intrinsic merit of the styles that inspire. Yet the contemporary problem of the academic is as real as the fact of death, whether it is the young musician who sounds more like a recording than an improvisor or the pretentious composer so in awe of 20th-century concert music that we are asked to suffer through third-rate Stravinsky, Schoenberg, Bartók, Messiaen, Stockhausen, and even the leftovers from the minimalist school—the last imitation especially surprising in face of the fact that the repeated melodic or rhythmic kernel known as the riff was a Kansas City dance-band building block fifty years ago!

What Dodge contributed in that essay, and in a later attack on the many critical pieces of one sort or another that had appeared by the time he wrote *Consider the Critics* in 1939, was the sense that jazz was at once a decidedly Western music but one that had developed its own instrumental, rhythmic, and harmonic styles. Dodge was limited largely to what he and many others called the "hot" style that grew to fruition by the middle 1920s; he was incapable of hearing the refinements that Ellington was making in a decidedly avant-garde way, just as he missed the point of bebop. But it is not the role of a critic to know everything or to be right at every instance. The job is to illuminate, and illumination is the true art of criticism. Dodge recognized the dangers of pretension, and he was smart enough to know that once techniques that were initially considered bizarre become part of a recognizable tradition, it is rank foolishness to pursue only the bizarre when there are true accomplishments from which to build new ideas. "The whole confused attitude towards Modern Art," he wrote in *Consider the Critics,* ". . . hung on one hook, and still hangs on it to a degree, that shock must prevail, that it is only from him who shocks that we may expect Modern Art!"

Yet when Dodge wrote *Harpsichords and Jazz Trumpets,* his discussion of the piano's potential was perhaps the most far-reaching of any jazz criticism written before the middle of the 50s. Thelonious Monk was seventeen years old when Dodge laid out a vision of the piano in jazz that had yet to emerge:

> Owing to the conspicuous commonplaces of our virtuosi, the negro pianist only too easily slips into the fluid superficialities of a Liszt cadenza. This tendency of the negro to imitate the florid piano music of the 19th century which he hears all around him, has kept the piano backward in finding its own Jazz medium. It takes a very developed musical sense to improvise significantly on the piano, a talent for thinking in more than one voice. The counterpoint that Jazz instruments achieve [in the] ensemble is possible to a certain extent on the piano alone, but this takes a degree of development Jazz has not yet reached. The best piano solos so far, in my opinion, are the melodic "breaks" imitating [the] trumpet and trombone. Lately the pianist has found some biting chords, and felt a new desire to break up melody, not only rhythmically as inspired by the drum, but rhythmically as a percussion instrument fundamentally inspired by its own peculiar harmonic percussion. This, perhaps, will lead him to contribute something no other musician has.

That is what I consider first-class jazz writing, because its insight into the future style of Thelonious Monk was based on the specifics of the idiom itself, rather than on an attempt to make it sound more European by reducing the aesthetic elements that made the music such a singular phenomenon in the first place.

What was wrong in 1939, when Dodge took on the abundance of flimsy ideas about the music, is still wrong. This problem, of course, is not exclusive to jazz. Like most American criticism, jazz writing is either too academic to communicate with any people other than professionals, or it is so inept in its enthusiasm or so cowardly in its willingness to submit to fashion that it has failed to gain jazz the respect among intelligent people necessary for its support as more than a popular art.

Unlike the European improvisation that Dodge described, jazz is primarily a performance art that takes place in an ensemble context of collective improvisation. Until the middle 1960s, the music's basic

vocabulary had to be redefined in a functional sense by every generation that could be considered innovative. Adventurous musicians had
to redefine the blues, four/four swing (fast, medium, and slow), the
ballad, and the Afro-Hispanic or "Latin" rhythm that Jelly Roll Morton suggested when he used the term "the Spanish tinge." Those were
technical requirements that had been in place at least since 1940, the
result of a continual wrestling with the problem of form perhaps
initiated by Buddy Bolden in New Orleans near the turn of the
century.

I think that those technical requirements demand that the jazz
writer know how to illuminate a given performance in terms suffi-
ciently specific to let the reader in on aesthetic thrills or to warn the
layman against ineptitude or fraud. These are the functions of all
intelligent criticism. And however much people such as LeRoi Jones
are obsessed with content over form, claiming that formal attention
is some version of Western imperialism dressed in aesthetic armor,
what made Louis Armstrong and every other important jazz musician
so significant to the music of this century was much more than feeling
or a susceptibility to uncontrolled trance; it was the ability to create
logical music on the wing, responding both to the structure at hand
and to the invention of his fellow players. Only the catatonic are
incapable of feeling, but what separates the artist from others is more
than the nature of his or her passion; it is the skill that allows an
interior human feeling to move all the way out into the world as an
objective artifact, replete with the synthesis of technical mastery and
expression that makes for all living, as opposed to academic, art.

So it is the illumination of the life, the vitality of the art, that is the
fundamental issue. Taste and opinion are always individual—or
should be—and every writer will prefer certain styles, instrumentalists, singers, and composers over others. What is essential, however, is integrity, an integrity based on as clear a perception of the
identity of the art as possible. Though there have almost always been
debates over the racial components of jazz, it is obviously an Afro-
American form, meaning that the irreplaceable force at the center of
its identity has been the musical imagination of the Negro. But this

fact does not imply that white musicians, listeners, and critics have no place in the making or the evaluation of the idiom. Its Afro-American essence isn't nullified by whites, any more than Jessye Norman's singing of Schubert or Leontyne Price's renditions of Puccini neutralize the German and Italian origins of those musics. Yet when I once heard Woody Herman say to Edwin Newman that jazz was initially the black man's music but white musicians made it universal, I wondered what the response would have been had a Negro performer of European concert music claimed that the idiom was originally the white man's music but black concert artists had made it universal!

Human meaning and human value are what make an idiom universal, nothing else. Specific stylistic elements are the things that create individual, idiomatic identity, and style is inevitably a code for the perception of human life and human meaning in a particular context. When Leontyne Price performs *Tosca*, what we observe is that Italian opera is so inclusive that a Negro from Laurel, Mississippi, can meet its requirements and express her own artistic identity as well.

Parallel truths are witnessed when we hear a white American play good jazz, or when we listen to a gypsy named Django Reinhardt light up the guitar with such authority on his recordings that we can understand why Duke Ellington, who took a backseat to no one in terms of ethnic pride, chose Reinhardt as his special guest for performances with the greatest idiomatic orchestra in the history of jazz. Consequently, to recognize the core component of the Negro when we discuss jazz is not to pander to genetic theories or to the superficial impositions of lightweight political theories; it is to recognize cultural facts too well documented to argue. America obviously has much to do with it, since no comparable so-called minority of African extraction has produced as internationally influential a body of artists, performers, athletes, entertainers, and even political visionaries as the United States. As Albert Murray observes in his extraordinary *Stomping the Blues*, "The synthesis of European and African musical elements in the West Indies, the Caribbean, and in continental Latin America produced calypso, rhumba, the tango, the conga, mambo, and so on, but not the blues and not ragtime, and not that extension, elaboration, and refinement of blues-break riffing and improvisation which came to be known as jazz." And no Africans in the history of the modern world have come to mean what Louis Armstrong and Duke Ellington symbolize in this century. Were it merely a matter of genetics, or even oppression, this would not be the case.

Armstrong, who is to jazz improvisation what the Wright Brothers were to aerodynamics, and Ellington, who is to jazz orchestration what D. W. Griffith was to the grammar of cinema, represent freedom, eloquence, discipline, lyricism, sexuality, joy, tragedy, ambivalence, and transcendent elegance as aesthetically expressed through jazz. They were the products of a culture so peculiar and so penetrating that it inspired converts far beyond the distinctions of skin tone. Though I fundamentally disagree with the conclusions that Martin Williams arrived at about the comparative quality of the Fletcher Henderson and Benny Goodman orchestras in a 1984 essay entitled "Just Asking," Williams raises some questions that are unavoidable when considering the influence of jazz and the quality of jazz criticism. As a white man near sixty who has been writing extremely well about jazz for at least thirty years, Williams asks questions about Goodman and about Mick Jagger. For the purpose of this discussion, I will only cite what he asks about Goodman, then quote his final questions about the success of both:

> Putting it in terms of my generation: why would it be that a young man growing up in Chicago in the teens of this century, the son of Russian Jewish immigrant parents, would want to learn to play the clarinet like a colored Creole from New Orleans named Jimmie Noone? Why would the act of doing that be so meaningful to him? And having done that, why would he then want to form an orchestra that played like that of an American mulatto from Georgia named Fletcher Henderson? And stake his career in music on doing that? And after that, why would the world make him a celebrity and one of the most famous musicians of the century?

> Of course there is the question of why mass audiences seemed to want to hear Goodman over Henderson and Jagger over Muddy Waters. But it

can't be blamed on Goodman that more people wanted to hear him than wanted to hear Chick Webb, or on Jagger that more people attended him than John Lee Hooker.

My question here is what drew Benny and Mick to make such music in the first place, and such large audiences to want to hear it at all? Both men obviously express something deeply, abidingly important to their followers. What is it?

Why do we all, at whatever level, find such meaning in the musical culture of Afro-Americans? Why has their music so triumphed throughout the world? We invoke it to get through our adolescence and most of us keep it, one way or another, central in our lives.

Those are the kinds of questions only a critic with integrity would ask, questions only a person committed to the high seriousness necessary to inform, challenge, and stimulate would publicly contemplate. One aspect of what Williams poses takes in the human level that is inextricably woven into the experience of artistic inspiration and communication, the other encompasses the relationship of race to American economic success. On one level, I think that the appeal of jazz has been its daring, its charming cockiness, its projection of individual human value as expressed in a collective context. There is also what I consider a double consciousness very different from the one described by Du Bois. What I refer to is the expression of sorrow or melancholy in a melodic line that is contrasted by a jaunty or exuberant rhythm, that combination of grace and intensity we know as swing. In jazz, sorrow rhythmically transforms itself into joy, which is perhaps the point of the music: joy earned or arrived at through performance, through creation.

That affirmative underpinning of swing has always been explicitly or implicitly connected to dance, but the appeal of Afro-American rhythm is much older than jazz, even older than the emergence of Frank Johnson's Colored Band. Joseph Marks, in *America Learns to Dance,* quotes an observer who was startled in 1789 when he saw some undergraduates at Princeton "dancing up and down the entry as a Negro played upon a violin with twenty students hallooing and tearing about." Since dancing is so important to every culture in some form or another, it is understandable that the group which we see inventing so many of the steps and so much of the music that goes with them would penetrate so deeply into the consciousness of the society. Beyond that, there is the fact that in the United States the technological elements that make for the modern age were developing in tandem with the complexity of social evolution that took place when the issue of democracy had to meet the multiracial components of American culture.

There is another fact that cannot be ignored in this discussion. Ours is a century in which percussion and polyrhythm are fundamental to its identity, in which the machinery of the age and the activities of the people parallel the multilinear densities and rhythms of the very rain forest that could easily have been the inspiration for Africa's drum choirs, with their broad sense of sound and their involvement with perpetual rhythmic motion. The celebratory rhythm of swing became a new kind of lyricism, a feeling that gave the drums a fundamental position in an art music that didn't disavow dance, a role in which set and improvised syncopation took on a fresh fluency. The result was that Negro Americans put the Western world on two and four, asserting a conception of time that created an uproar when Stravinsky emulated the accents of a ragtime band in his *Rite of Spring*. As Wynton Marsalis points out, "Stravinsky turned European music over with a backbeat. Check it out. What they thought was weird and primitive was just a Negro beat on the bass drum."

I would also submit that cinematic cross-cutting is not only percussive but antiphonal, a visual call and response as indispensable to modern imagery as it has always been to Negro field hollers, church music, and jazz improvisation. Further, I would say that the close-up parallels the jazz solo, the featured voice. In fact Fred Astaire, perhaps the most famous and successful American dancer of the century, became a screen star by often using the Negro pedal percussion of tap dance and performing most of his numbers to Tin Pan Alley songs such as *Top Hat* that could not have arrived without the inspiration of Negro melody and phrasing. And considering that James Reese Europe collaborated with Vernon and Irene Castle, writing the music for the dances they popularized and inventing the fox-trot and the turkey trot, we can see with clarity a line easily traceable back to 1789, when those Princeton students began to shake their cakes to the intoxicating music of the Negro. Combine all those elements with the Negro American vision of infinite plasticity as expressed in the democratic ensemble of the jazz band, and I believe that you have the answer to Williams's question about the overwhelming appeal of Afro-American musical culture.

The subject of white success over that of black is grating and sobering, sometimes depressing, but the fact that soars above all those inequities is that the lasting aesthetic achievements of black musicians haven't been lessened by the taste of the public. The thrill one experiences in listening to the recordings Count Basie's band made when it came roaring out of Kansas City to redefine swing and elevate the thrust and depth of the rhythm section isn't minimized by the differences in Basie's and Goodman's paychecks. What we can actually draw great comfort from is an incredible victory for dedication, knowing that Negro musicians, regardless of what could have been discouraging career obstacles, continued to create splendid music that has withstood, as all true art does, the inexorable passage of time.

We can explain the public preference for Goodman by simply citing racism. We could further that by noting that the sexual energy which always curls and pulsates somewhere inside dance was more easily accepted, matinee-idol style, when the music that provoked those movements was played by white bands. We needn't even agree with Freud to use his area of speculation as an acknowledgment of the truth that sexuality is far from simple; nor, at this point, do we have to pretend that the sexual access of and to Negro men has not inspired much of the violence at the most furious end of racist practices. Discrimination always maintains a who's who in the boudoir. That, perhaps, explains why Caucasians playing Afro-American styles have often been more popular than the artistic merits of their own works would objectively indicate.

As far as the Mick Jaggers, Cyndi Laupers, and Bruce Springsteens are concerned, unlike LeRoi Jones, I'm not particularly interested in the careers of pop stars, nor do I care about black recording labels such as Motown that showed no affinity for jazz. Even the question of racism seems no more the point, especially since a rail-tailed Negro named Michael Jackson sold more copies of a single album than any singer or instrumentalist in recorded history; or a blind Negro named Stevie Wonder has earned more dollars than the most popular composers and instrumentalists in both jazz and European concert music; or a horse-faced Negro from the South named Lionel Richie pulls down millions for songs that contain so little melodic, harmonic, and rhythmic character that even the most imaginative jazz musicians haven't tried to use them as bridges to a larger audience in the way they could when the best of Tin Pan Alley was in flower.

What I am concerned about, and what I see as the task facing the serious writer about jazz, is how the literature on the music might help create a following for the art in this country that would parallel the listening public which European concert music has. I say "in this country" because jazz musicians do very well outside this country—the best ones, the journeymen, the mediocre, and even the fakes. But in the United States, since jazz is no longer the popular music it was fifty years ago, the problem is getting its aesthetic richness appreciated by all who consider themselves sophisticated and civilized. Again, unlike European concert music, the idiom hasn't inspired the support of wealthy patrons (black or white), the erection of concert halls, or quality explanation in the most prestigious musical institutions across the country. This is where the battle for jazz writing really lies—not in the arena of popular music. Our era is characterized by a lack of interest in variation and by a love of repetition that dominates the sound of popular music, making it much harder for the jazz musician to achieve the attention of the listener. Ironically, the appetite for mindless trance states that LeRoi Jones celebrates can best be witnessed in the world's discos. Perhaps this is why some people say that Hitler was the first rock star; his message inspired the masses of Germany to turn their backs on the complex demands of modern life in favor of brutish primitivism. As André Hodeir wrote in *Toward Jazz*, "the crowd's need to be convinced is the nose by which it is most easily led. The millions of addlepates who cheered Hitler on the eve of World War were expressing and sharing an absolute conviction; many of them died before they could realize that their enthusiasm reflected nothing more than abysmal feeblemindedness."

So the jazz writer has a big job, a task that demands illuminating an idiom dominated by adult passion in an era overshadowed by an international appetite for adolescent obsessiveness. Living in a world where adults too frequently look upon teenagers as sages, we must know we are no longer in a jazz age; the music that first took virtuoso flight on the wings of Louis Armstrong's imagination dispensed with sentimentality, spoke as directly and as ambivalently about adult sexuality as *Ulysses,* and allowed for the perpetual rejuvenation of material through the process of improvisation. It is the art of grown men and grown women, which was part of its appeal and part of its attraction to the young musicians who were bitten by the night creature of jazz. In order to serve this idiom, we must speak of it with the insights expected of adults, not some one-dimensional fervor for a beat, not some savage attraction to frothing intensity that fails to express the bittersweet stretch of human feeling, and not some political theory that reduces a long march of heroic achievement to checkers on a board of supposed scientific materialism.

At this point, after many years of avant-garde frauds and sellouts to the rock-and-roll god of fusion, we are lucky to see a growing number of young musicians, most of them black, who are committing themselves to jazz. Wynton Marsalis has been an extraordinary catalyst in this resurgence of interest among young musicians in jazz, but he is only an indication of what is now taking place. Every few months, another young man or woman, black or white, arrives in New York expressing the ambition to swing and to meet the artistic standards set by the music's greatest practitioners. This is something that all of us who believe in jazz must be grateful for, because the vast majority of those who were considered avant-garde twenty years ago represented the first generation in the history of the art who were incapable of meeting the technical standards set by their predecessors. Unlike Charlie Parker, who could play with anyone, or John Coltrane, who so mastered his tradition that even Johnny Hodges admired his work on the recording Coltrane made with Duke Ellington, these supposed avant-garde players arrogantly described their narrow skills as expressive of stylistic advances. But history and aesthetic standards are now manhandling the bulk of them, though others still escape under the cover of arguments bootlegged from the world of cultural anthropology, where relative value is trumpeted as a shield against racism.

To achieve the respect for the idiom that it deserves, the jazz writer must accurately perceive real mastery as opposed to rhetorical compensations for incompetence, and should know the difference between thorough contributions to jazz and the submissions to pop trends or the pretensions to European avant-gardism that shape the work of those talented but misled musicians incapable of inventing fresh directions within the parameters of the jazz tradition. In considering the attempt to make something of value out of the mire Miles Davis pushed jazz into, we should remember what Roger Pryor Dodge wrote of the premiere of *Rhapsody in Blue:*

> February 12 now stood for two births, that of Abraham Lincoln and the *Rhapsody in Blue*. Critics, whose business was sharp musical observation, succumbed to the reasoning that something vital must have occurred since a concert crowd roared. Even those sympathetic to Gershwin's bathos, but trained enough to recognize and comment upon the inept handling of the completely familiar concerto form, followed the line of least resistance.

And as far as those who claim to be working at the frontiers of the art are concerned, we should be aware of what Hodeir wrote of Thelonious Monk in 1959: "Monk's solution, though related in some ways to the formal conceptions of serious modern music, is not indebted, for its guiding principles, to any school of music, past or present, which is foreign to jazz; this, I feel, is essential." Regardless of what quarrels one might have with certain other ideas of Hodeir's, he hit the appropriate afterbeat in the perpetual rhythm of dialogue between this art and its commentary. If we examine what is presented as innovative, it is our responsibility to also understand what Hodeir meant when he wrote in the same essay, "Ten years of mediocre row music have taught us that discontinuity can, at times, be no more than an alibi for incoherence." Alibis can never stand in for the truths of artistic beauty, and if we are to spread the word on jazz with any authority, we must know the difference between them.

Billy Taylor, *Presenter*

Jazz in the Contemporary Marketplace: Professional and Third-Sector Economic Strategies for the Balance of the Century

These are, at once, the best and worst times for jazz. This important indigenous music is recognized as a unique American contribution to world culture. Its many varied styles, its huge repertoire, and its idealization of the concept of individual freedom, combined with spontaneous creativity, have created a large group of world-class jazz musicians who participate in concerts, festivals, broadcasts, recordings, and other musical and cultural activities on an international scale. The efforts of experienced jazz musicians as performers, recording artists, teachers, clinicians, and role models have resulted in the development of several generations of outstanding young jazz artists. The Voice of America has identified, educated, and entertained a large, worldwide jazz audience. It broadcasts many hours of jazz on a daily basis and sends both live and recorded programs to faithful listeners all over the globe. National Public Radio and American Public Radio have provided similar services on a national basis.

Despite all this growth in the exposure of the music, the support services for jazz have not kept pace with the creative efforts of hardworking, dedicated professionals in the field. Why does this situation exist when we have so much to work with? We could start at home. There is a large reservoir of experienced and talented professional jazz musicians living in all parts of the United States, who perform on a high level of musicality when given the opportunity. Many of these creative artists teach, so they are constantly sharing their insights with aspiring jazz musicians. As a result, there is an even larger group of well-trained amateur and semiprofessional musicians emerging. They are ready, willing, and able to join the established professionals who are working hard to take jazz to its next stage of development. What must be done to help these artists fulfill their potential? Perhaps we should begin by examining some of the available resources.

Many colleges and universities function as cultural centers, providing learning opportunities, rehearsal space, performance space, and opportunities to work with artists in other disciplines. In addition to well-defined jazz courses offered by institutions such as Berklee College of Music, North Texas State University, Indiana University, the University of Wisconsin, the University of Miami, and the University of Massachusetts, jazz is being taught and performed in a wide range of performing arts high schools, settlement schools, private music schools, music stores, churches, and cultural centers of all kinds, resulting in a tremendous growth of interest in the music and the artists who create it.

There are other reasons for the growth of interest in jazz. The well-publicized tours of famous jazz artists; consistent exposure to their records and their personal performances; special presentations and initiatives taken by organizations such as Jazzmobile, the National Jazz Service Organization, the National Association of Jazz Educators, the International Association of Jazz, the Charlie Parker Memorial Foundation, and hundreds of jazz societies; jazz tours, trips, and activities sponsored by radio stations and corporations; and the innumerable efforts put forth by a few nightclub owners, indomitable fans, and a handful of knowledgeable and dedicated people in the recording business, have done much to aid the development of jazz. Other contributions and factors include the efforts of those who write about jazz, program it, promote it, manage the artists, and document its history and development. These efforts have led to more educational jazz festivals, more city-sponsored jazz festivals, more corporate involvement in the sponsorship of jazz activities, the organization of many jazz repertory orchestras, and the establishment of new venues for jazz performances (such as parks, city streets, arcades between buildings, piers, bandwagons, and so on). The new venues take on added importance with the demise of traditional jazz theaters and nightclubs.

Because of the difficulties they have experienced breaking into the field or maintaining creative control over their musical presentations, many jazz musicians have been forced to create their own job opportunities by renting clubs, concert halls, and other facilities in order to present their music the way they conceive it. Many are also establishing their own music publishing companies and recording companies for the same reasons. Some have found ways to interact with singers, dancers, choreographers, and filmmakers in creating new works of art. Others have established liaisons with business organizations who use them to promote products. Indeed, endorsing musical instruments has helped the careers of many jazz musicians, and this activity has been greatly stimulated by new technology such as digital sampling synthesizers and sequencers, which process a wide variety of sounds that can be programmed for replay and recording (including drum machines, machines that simulate strings' sounds, brass sounds, reed sounds, vocal sounds, and much more).

The new technology has opened a new musical frontier, but it has also caused some serious problems: machines are replacing live musicians in the recording studios and in some types of live performances. In spite of this there is a resurgence of interest in acoustic playing.

Perhaps the most important reason for the growth of interest in jazz is that our society is evolving from an industrial economy into an information and services economy. In this context the relationship of the arts to all of society is more important than it has ever been.

In his unpublished paper "The Arts: A Vocabulary for the New Economy," Dominick Attanasio, vice president for planning and business development of Pfizer, Inc., notes that once productivity allows members of a society to satisfy their basic needs for food and shelter, an increasing portion of discretionary income becomes available for the satisfaction of inner needs. He further states that increasingly more economic behavior is motivated not by the need for things—the classic consumables and durables of agriculture and industrial economies—but by the desire for certain kinds of experience. More people are asking "What do I want to experience?" instead of "What do I want to have?"

At its best, jazz has always provided an unusually satisfying experience because it involves the artists and the audience in types of interplay that greatly enhance the art of spontaneous creativity. Pianist Erroll Garner used to say that the audience was the fourth member of his trio, and today many contemporary jazz musicians seem much more interested in communicating with their audience than they once were. The audience also seems to be changing its attitude toward the artists and responding more readily to a wide variety of jazz styles. Realizing this, many jazz musicians are doing their best to break down stylistic barriers and challenging themselves and their audiences with the results of their experimentation. The fusion of Latin, East Indian, and other ethnic elements with jazz has attracted new listeners who are seeking music less predictable and more melodically and harmonically satisfying than most pop and rock music. Many singers have included the compositions of jazz composers in their shows and on their recordings, thus exposing the music to pop, soul, country, and Latin music fans.

Unfortunately, this trend has been misunderstood and misused by recording and concert producers. Guided by the desire to make large profits quickly, many of them have used the same big-name artists over and over, until their box-office value has been diminished. They have then moved on to exploit other big-name artists, consistently ignoring the need (from a business as well as an artistic point of view) to build the next generation of attractions. This inexcusable practice needs to be discontinued and the situation rectified as soon as possible. The presentation of jazz is a highly profitable business when one counts all the receipts, so better business practices should be adopted.

When the business potential of jazz is carefully examined, it becomes apparent that too much time, talent, and resources are wasted. A large worldwide audience has been identified, but it has often been badly exploited rather than carefully and thoughtfully developed. This situation can be corrected if enough knowledgeable, concerned, creative, and talented people come together and develop workable plans of action that will bring to the jazz art form the kinds of educational, cultural, and business support that will help it achieve financial stability and ensure its continued growth and development.

Currently, jazz needs special attention and comprehensive support because the field has been segmented into many arbitrary styles. It has been consistently treated as a small, special, underground music that has its own mystique and its own small audience. It has been poorly presented, underadvertised, and given little of the consistent exposure and business opportunities common to other fields (rock and soul, for example). How many jazz artists receive large sums of money to pay for rehearsal and studio time so that they can develop a concept? How many jazz artists get promotional tours, full-page ads in trade papers, posters, media hype, and in-store promotions for their recordings? How many recording companies keep jazz discs or tapes in print beyond the first one or two small releases? How many companies recognize the historical importance and long-term sales potential of the artists they record?

The problems I am pointing out are well known, and they need to be resolved for everyone's benefit. I would like to offer a few other suggestions. First, existing organizations should provide a well-defined entry point into the jazz field—a place where a musician could receive helpful career counseling, guidance, and support (much of the advice currently given is inadequate and ineffective because it is based on outdated and narrow views of the jazz field). Talented musicians, young and old, should be provided with a place to submit tapes for criticism, plus original compositions, musical concepts, and audition tapes. A pipeline should be developed that would lead to the publication of the best music and the recording and proper merchandising of the widest variety of jazz.

Meet the Composer, Inc., could be helpful in developing this idea. This program's handbook on the commissioning of new works and its many projects with performing rights societies, corporations, and nonprofit organizations have given it unparalleled experience in this area. The Jazzmobile Workshop/Clinic could also serve as a model for a place where aspiring musicians who have neither the time nor the money to study privately or in a music school could develop or sharpen their musical and performance skills. The National Jazz Service Organization could broaden its technical assistance program, which helps artists obtain support for their careers through already existing channels and encourages them to develop alternatives.

The jazz field needs to consistently attract and develop managers, lawyers, accountants, business advisers, producers, publicists, and presenters who are responsive to the needs of jazz artists and capable of assisting them in structuring viable careers. There are, of course, outstanding, effective individuals in each of these categories already, but jazz needs many more. We could certainly use a larger group of sensitive and capable professionals who could be hired to work with individual artists, as well as ensembles, through every stage of their career development. A central place for contact in this area is also necessary.

Among our other underused resources are the elder statesmen and stateswomen of jazz. A national program should be established to honor the many artists who have made tremendous contributions to the art form. This should not be a popularity contest, but rather a unified and concerted effort to allow the entire jazz field to benefit from their wisdom. There are many living musicians who have helped create and codify jazz; they should be given the opportunity to share their experiences and insights with aspiring artists and interested audiences. Roy Eldridge, Benny Carter, Max Roach, Milt

Hinton, and many other great artists have done this for years on their own, but there should be a national program that would make the information they have to share available to a broader, more diversified audience. This is an activity that could be centered in the National Center for Jazz currently being considered by the National Jazz Service Organization. Audiotape, videotape, and laser technology should be used to store and disseminate the recollections and historical perspective supplied by these artists. Collections such as those housed in the Institute for Jazz Studies at Rutgers University, the Smithsonian Institution, and the Schomburg Center for Research in Black Culture should be expanded and used more effectively by a larger proportion of the jazz field. Much of my work in this area has been taped by schools and the media, so I assume there is already a large body of material available from others, which needs to be collected, collated, and made available to a wider audience. The National Endowment for the Arts' Jazz Masters Awards are an excellent beginning, but this concept should be expanded and given more support and visibility.

There are many cities throughout the nation that have nurtured the talents of great jazz artists. They should regularly celebrate the contributions of local and regional jazz artists with programs that stimulate greater awareness and appreciation of the important part they have played in adding new dimensions to the music. New York, Chicago, Kansas City, Detroit, Philadelphia, and New Orleans have taken the lead with Jazzmobile, Chicago-Fest, the Kansas City Jazz Commission, Jazz Reach, the Jazz and Heritage Festival, and other programs that have done much to propagate jazz. New York and Washington, D.C., have been among the first cities to use professional jazz artists regularly as a part of their Sister City cultural exchanges. This idea could be greatly expanded and further improved.

We should use the existing documentation of the continuing contributions of women to the jazz field to integrate their efforts more effectively into every aspect of the art form. The National Jazz Service Organization could offer models that could be expanded and adapted to address this problem.

A broad-based effort should be made to incorporate jazz into the daily lives of the general public. Every possible aspect of the electronic and print media should be used to the fullest extent. We must develop media programs that reflect, as accurately as possible, the spirit of the music and the intent of the musician. The National Jazz Service Organization should initiate a regular series of seminars to assemble serious jazz writers, musicians, media people, publicists, record promoters, and others who are involved in helping the public form opinions on jazz. They should devise better ways to report more regularly, more accurately, and more objectively on the activities that are important both to the jazz field and to the public. We need to present our case better through existing channels and we need to call attention to those in media who are already helping and support them more effectively. Even though the *Rolling Stone Jazz Record Guide* gives a clear indication of the importance *others* attach to our music, we should be doing more of this kind of documentation *ourselves*.

Since jazz has traditionally been documented on records, there is a great need for trained professionals in every aspect of the recording business who understand and relate to its special qualities. Jazz is an important element in the growth of cassette and compact disc sales. The impact of the compact disc on the recording industry demonstrates quite clearly that jazz fans will spend large quantities of money for the music they like. The expanded playing time provided on cassettes was important to them, and the digital sound of compact discs took the next step toward better fidelity. Digital audiotape and compact videodiscs are adding further flexibility in this direction.

A great need exists for more music publishers who will follow the lead of Jamey Aebersold and produce jazz publications that are well-conceived, accurate, attractive, and available to those who want to play it, study it, or just learn about it. There should be more stores throughout the country selling educational and performance material designed specifically for people interested in learning about jazz.

Inexpensive rehearsal spaces and better venues for jam sessions and experimental jazz activities are needed. Jazz musicians need comfortable and congenial places in which to work on performance problems and overcome obstacles that only surface during the heat of performance. Producers of recordings and jazz events could use such jam sessions and rehearsals to train sound and light technicians to properly mike and light the musicians and thus enhance the performances. They could also use these occasions to broaden their own perspectives and sharpen their programming and production ideas.

Since there is already a great deal of jazz activity taking place in schools and cultural centers, more focused efforts should be made to integrate this indigenous music into existing educational programs. Efforts to use jazz musicians as artists-in-residence, music teachers, composers-in-residence, music directors, conductors, and consultants should be studied, documented, and improved. An American jazz school directory similar to that published by the Association of Hungarian Musicians and the Hungarian section of the International Jazz Federation should be published and made available to students who wish to compare schools and the jazz courses they offer. The directory should list schools, courses, requirements, length of courses, fees, degrees offered, instructors, and other pertinent information.

A directory of jazz collections should also be published, listing where they are, what they are, and how available they are to scholars and the general public. The same directory could list nonprofit and for-profit jazz-related organizations and include information on their programs and activities. Museums and other places that collect, house, and display jazz memorabilia, tapes, records, photos, and books should be a part of this directory.

There needs to be a concentrated effort to market and distribute jazz performances more effectively. This effort should be directed to live performances and performances on radio and television, as well as performances on records, tapes, and video. Well-informed, open-minded radio executives, personalities, programmers, and salespeople could be extremely helpful in this endeavor. Everyone involved should know as much as possible about the music, the musicians, and the total audience and be prepared to do what is necessary to involve all of them more fully. If this is done properly, there will be more jazz on commercial radio and television—because it will be profitable to put it there.

Organizations such as Jazzmobile, National Jazz Service Organization, National Association of Jazz Educators, International Association of Jazz, and other qualified nonprofit jazz organizations should be given more support by public and private funding sources. Their successful programs should be documented, expanded, used as models, and replicated. In this way, activities such as free outdoor jazz concerts, workshops, clinics, lecture/demonstrations, special jazz events and celebrations, seminars, jazz festivals and parties, and other outreach activities could be improved and expanded. Similar activities organized and presented by jazz societies should also be supported. These organizations have long been recognized as the most ardent, faithful, and vocal supporters of jazz and jazz musicians. Their energy and commitment should be harnessed more effectively.

John Swenson, editor of the *Rolling Stone Jazz Record Guide,* has stated that

> Jazz is a vital piece of American history—but nowadays it is too often viewed as a rarefied special interest, especially by the recording industry. But as rock music has moved further into the realm of fashionmongering, shortsightedly attempting to become soundtrack music for video, it has abandoned an audience that once looked to it for qualities of emotional commitment—what can generally be called soul. Now these listeners have turned in even greater numbers to jazz, a music that has championed the essence of soul throughout its existence.

Jazz is on the threshold of a significant breakthrough. If the field is properly motivated, mobilized, and organized, the music can be put into an excellent position of growth and stability. The talent is there, the audience is there, the business acumen is there. We need to fuse those three elements and raise jazz to its proper level of acceptance, support, and financial stability.

Jazz in the Contemporary Marketplace: Professional and Third-Sector Economic Strategies for the Balance of the Century

Billy Taylor has prepared a very thorough paper on the situation that now exists in the uniquely American art form called jazz. As he states in his first line, "These are, at once, the best and worse times for jazz."

My own devotion to this music—mainstream jazz—has been with me for over fifty years. Not knowing one note from another, and not ever wanting to learn music, I have dedicated nearly a lifetime to help in every way I can to promote and present jazz. Starting as a jazz disc jockey in the days when you could play jazz records on AM radio, I devoted those years to playing favorites. I helped launch the careers of Stan Kenton, Dizzy Gillespie, Charlie Parker, Mel Tormé, André Previn, Dave Brubeck, Paul Desmond, and others. I was proud to have known and been known by Duke, Bill Basie, Nat Cole, Ella, Erroll Garner, John Lewis, George Shearing, Sarah, Woody, Joe Williams, and many, many more.

These people were and are the inspiration behind the Monterey Jazz Festival. Thirty years ago I realized that they could be the ones who could contribute greatly to my interest in promoting and preserving this music. I talked to local fans and businessmen and convinced them to help by providing a nonprofit educational corporation to present a festival with the best in mainstream jazz.

So in 1958 I started what is now the oldest continuing jazz festival in the world, with all proceeds going into jazz education. The 1986 budget alone for jazz education was $80,000, and the total we have invested in this pursuit so far is nearly $1 million. The best high school jazz players in California will perform on my Sunday afternoon program with a number of professionals. They were selected by a panel of pros from hundreds of youngsters who tried out from all over the state for one of the twenty chairs. They come to Monterey for a full week of rehearsal under the direction of Bill Berry, with help from other artists who will be there. Over the past sixteen years we have had this regular feature, and many students have later received scholarships to the Berklee, Interlochen, and Dick Grove schools. This phase of our efforts has been the most important to me.

During the school year itself, we have visiting professionals making the rounds of Monterey County high schools and junior high schools every three weeks. This is our major thrust. That, plus presenting major talents to 6,800 sold-out seats for the last seven years. Talents, that is, who play mainstream jazz.

Too many jazz festivals, as I see it, don't stick to this philosophy. They try to appeal to a bigger audience by presenting "names" with a bigger gate attraction, all in the pursuit of dollars. I personally find this practice denigrating to the word "jazz."

All this, of course, is an expression of how we make our contribution to the art form of jazz. We know our efforts are meaningful in our small part of the entire picture, but what about "for the balance of the century" and beyond?

Billy Taylor speaks of all the resources available. Musicians, educators, and other professionals in the business should certainly have a central clearinghouse for directing the future of jazz. Certainly it is time to do as he suggests: integrate this indigenous music into educational programs supplemented by directories, recorded collections, and marketing efforts. During my time in radio, working at stations from 100 to 50,000 watts, I programmed only jazz. In those days, however, all were AM stations, and FM was only starting. Today, what AM station plays jazz?

Taylor's suggestions are all valid. The only question that remains is who will organize, collate, and get the support needed to bring all these ideas to reality? Will it in truth be a program for NJSO? I believe that he has summarized his entire paper in his final paragraph, and I agree wholeheartedly.

One addendum: In a recent *San Francisco Chronicle,* Dr. Herb Wong, a leader of the National Association of Jazz Educators and a recording producer now with his own label, Black Hawk, stated, "Jazz isn't dead at all. Its festivals and concerts are developing the new jazz audience. All the major recording labels are getting back into jazz. It's the classical music of our country. The future of jazz is extremely bright."

Jazz in the Contemporary Marketplace: Professional and Third-Sector Economic Strategies for the Balance of the Century

When a lady in the audience once complained that she didn't understand what Miles Davis was playing, he responded, according to Duke Ellington's book *Music Is My Mistress*, with one of the sage statements on the art: "It took me twenty years' study and practice to work up to what I wanted to play in this performance. How can she expect to listen five minutes and understand it?"

In discussing strategies for increasing the commercial viability of jazz in the contemporary marketplace, we should consider how music in general, and jazz in particular, are perceived by both the artist and the audience. As America's great contribution to world culture, jazz is today universally recognized as an art. Functioning as such, it is both a response to the environment and the times in which it is created, and a catalyst for change. As music and as art, we say it has "meaning." It means, ultimately, the society of which it is a product. Music/art/jazz, then, is of necessity at least a two-part process, involving creation of a work by an artist and a response to it by an audience. Whatever the artist's intentions, what counts in the final analysis is the audience's perception of and reaction to the work.

Unfortunately for jazz, there is a great gulf between the musical and the unmusical; and most of the world, it seems, is unmusical. Not, of course, in the sense of not wanting music, but rather, in the words of author/composer Anthony Burgess, "in a diffused incapacity to understand the nature of music." While, on the one hand, popular culture in particular wants nothing to do with art, the inflationary use of "artist," like that of "genius," has devalued the term in a music industry catering to pop culture, where it is applied to everyone indiscriminately. Clearly, the prevailing widespread ignorance of jazz among those for whom it should be most intelligible is the result of a failure to communicate. And jazz, as well as music in general, art, and culture, could benefit from a more attentive and responsible cultivation (read "education") of American audiences.

Much, if indeed not most, of the responsibility for this failure to communicate jazz to a larger audience lies not with the artists (though they are by no means totally absolved here) but with the audiences themselves and especially with the promoters and programmers who consistently promote certain styles of music over others—that is, tunes that lack complexity and are unchallenging, emotionally thin, and intellectually insubstantial. Such pandering caters to and encourages an already cultivated laziness on the part of American audiences, the majority of whom would rather watch television game shows than read a book.

Even in a stepped-up program of audience education, the relatively little information that could be passed along in workshops and seminars alone might not be enough to reverse this trend. To be able to "hear" what one listens to comes from years of listening and years of living, a process of musical maturing and acquiring experience in general.

The fundamental premise is that the ability to hear the musicality of any group of sounds is key to determining our individual musical preferences. According to psychologist, musician, and author John

Booth Davies, "People engaged in actively listening to music are simultaneously doing two things: looking backward into the past and forward into the future." As Davies explains in *The Psychology of Music,* the "looking backward" involves the processing of information (that is, musical sounds) just heard, while "looking forward" involves anticipating what is most likely to happen next. The success of our "predictions" in this regard affects the way we feel about a piece of music, and is in large measure dependent upon how well we have processed the data or musical information available at any given point. People make tunes when they listen to music by exercising certain mental abilities that they possess. Listening to a tune is therefore not a passive process of mere reception, but one of active construction—recognizing basic units and structures, and organizing notes, patterns, and tonal sequences into groups or wholes, each constituting a psychological phrase.

The person with a fund of experience in ways of organizing particular types of material upon which to draw (for example, the veteran jazz fan) is at a distinct advantage when it comes to actually hearing (that is, making musical sense of) what he or she is listening to. In learning to appreciate music in the European classical tradition (and I use the term "classical" broadly to encompass the classical, baroque, rococo, Renaissance, romantic, and other movements as well), one is first familiarized, usually as a child, with simple piano works of Chopin; only gradually, over years of listening, does one eventually mature into an appreciation of Wagner and Schoenberg. The jazz tradition, too, has evolved along a continuum of increasing complexity, and it does not make sense to expect audiences to grasp Cecil Taylor who have not first understood Billy Taylor, Thelonious Monk, Bud Powell, and Fats Waller. We do not hear the music of Wynton Marsalis as an isolated phenomenon but as an outgrowth of Miles Davis, Dizzy Gillespie, Roy Eldridge, and Louis Armstrong.

Just as classical compositions have found their way into the popular lexicon via the lyricist (Borodin's *Polovtsian Dances* as *Stranger in Paradise* and Debussy's *Rêverie* as *My Reverie* being but two of many), so too have many jazz compositions found a larger public as a result of the accessibility that seems to accrue to the attachment of words to them—what, for example, King Pleasure did for *Moody's Mood for Love*. Many listeners who would normally claim not to like jazz find they can nevertheless enjoy James Moody's original instrumental version of this tune, perhaps because the subsequent lyric version has given them a reference point for making musical sense of his (Moody's) phrasing. Now, in the absence of words, they hear, perhaps for the first time, an "attitude" of the lyric echoed in the intonation and phrasing of the saxophone.

The "attitude" and other impressions we get from music become attached to it through a learning process. In the "Darling, they're playing our song" phenomenon, a specific emotional response is acquired for a tune that was heard when some other pleasurable business was taking place. In Pavlovian fashion, that past pleasurable experience becomes associated with the tune and is experienced again upon hearing the tune again. When a generation of listeners identifies a tune with a particularly agreeable period of their past, such a tune is likely to become a "classic" or "standard."

Advertising regularly plays off these kinds of emotional responses to music, as do films. Through this same process of association we learn to feel excitement and fear upon hearing an eerie tune at a horror movie, which we recognize instantly to be the calling card of the monster. Printed programs distributed at concerts, album liner notes and, of course, composition titles all function to suggest the mood that is appropriate to a piece of music. Long before Eddie Jefferson put lyrics to Miles Davis's composition *So What*, jazz fans heard the disyllabic phrase "so what" in the two-note response of the horns to Paul Chambers's bass lines. And a familiarity with Miles's personal mystique as it relates to the attitude of a phrase like "so what" can contribute to an even deeper understanding of the tune.

"We expect artists, like scientists, to be forward-looking, to fly in the face of what is established, and to create not what is accepted but what will become accepted," Jacob Bronowski pointed out in *A Sense of the Future*. "One result of the prizing of originality is that the artist now shares the unpopularity of the scientist: the large public dislikes and fears the way that both of them look at the world." Music that deviates significantly from particular stylistic norms, as does jazz from the popular song form, is less predictable and therefore has a higher information content for the listener to process. For the listener who is unfamiliar with the deviant form, processing the information, predicting where it will lead, and thus making musical sense of it will be difficult. On the other hand, a tune that a listener finds too familiar, and therefore too predictable, will have little information. He or she will perceive it as a tune, that is, as making musical sense but remaining extremely naive and boring.

According to Davies, two components that contribute to a person's musical preference are "interestingness" and "pleasingness," with optimum enjoyment being found in music that is, for any given listener, just slightly more interesting than pleasing. It may be for this reason, at least in part, that musical experience is a continuous process, a growing process, for most people. In Davies's words, "Music which an individual finds highly complex at first may become less complex with the passage of time and the acquisition of new musical experiences. . . . The subjective complexity level for any given piece of music *must* decline the more times it is played for the same listener." And further, "the hedonic value of complex musical stimuli increases with familiarity, while simple tunes with low information content will quickly reach a level at which they are no longer preferred."

> It cannot be emphasized too strongly that art, as such, does not pay . . . and that art that has to pay its own way is apt to become vitiated and cheap.—Antonín Dvořák

> There should be a single art exchange in the world, to which the artist could simply send his works and be given in return as much as he needs. As it is, one has to be half a merchant on top of everything else, and how badly one goes about it!—Ludwig van Beethoven, in a letter to Anton Hoffmeister, January 15, 1801

What jazz needs, it seems to me, is a strategy for saturating the airways. As sacrilegious as it may sound, Muzak versions of *Donna Lee, Monk's Dream, Giant Steps,* and other jazz classics flooding elevators, dentists' offices, and malls across the country, stretching that tiny space between the ears of American pop culture, might not be such a bad idea. What jazz really needs is the kind of "heavy rotation" on radio that pop, rock, and soul have gotten for more than thirty years now. Jazz needs more infiltration into the rock and soul stations on commercial radio, like that being provided by Hal Jackson (WBLS) and a few others.

If I may rephrase a statement from Dr. Taylor's paper, I predict that there will be more jazz on commercial radio and television *when* it becomes profitable to put it there. The trick, ultimately, will be to put it there—as much of it as possible—on speculation. Commercial radio, more than any single other factor, holds the key to making jazz profitable, not only for the few exceptional talents and <u>fortunate mediocrities</u> the media have chosen to spotlight, but profitable for the art form in general, as rock and roll is profitable. How many times have you caught yourself whistling something you didn't even like (and could not envision as having the least commercial potential) because you heard it on every radio station over and over again, everywhere you went? How many times have you looked back soberly and wondered how some groups could ever have achieved a hit? Like the Monkees?! Media saturation, and in the case of the Monkees, television, can truly work wonders.

Where the general public is concerned, this should be our primary focus, at least initially. We don't need to reinforce in the public's mind an association of jazz with the necessity of study and a great effort to understand and enjoy it, before we have even gotten their interest. More than anything, jazz needs exposure. If it consistently got the same kind of exposure on radio that rock and soul get, it would soon become as familiar, and as accessible.

The young adults who are graduating from high school today are probably the first generation whose parents listen to rock and who consequently did not grow up with jazz being played in the home.

Long before they had ever heard of jazz, children of the 1950s heard Cab Calloway's music as the background to Betty Boop cartoons on television. Animation artists today could find no more inspiring music than jazz to illustrate with visual images, the way Disney did with Stravinsky and others in *Fantasia*. This could be done at a fraction of the expense incurred in music videos; rather than competing with the outlandish antics and costumes of rock musicians, jazz artists could let their music, enhanced by the animation, speak for itself.

Jazz today is caught in a vicious cycle in which radio and recordings have programmed a simple-minded music to appeal to a mass market—the lowest common denominator. In so doing, they have cultivated an audience that is prejudiced against and largely incapable of comprehending anything more substantial than that which is regularly programmed for it. Commercial radio won't play jazz because their audience doesn't like it; the audience doesn't like it because it hasn't been exposed to it enough to begin to understand it. The recording companies can't afford to promote it if the audience is not buying it. Audiences will indeed have to be educated, but the much larger audience that jazz is now looking for will first have to be *attracted*. And it is the music, ultimately, that must be the attraction.

There must be a concentrated, collaborative effort on the part of recording companies, radio programmers, promoters, managers, musicians, publicists, jazz organizations, support groups, and schools to market and distribute more effectively. I would guarantee that if all the jazz fans in this country wrote letters to their local television stations today, jazz would be on television tomorrow. Jazz organizations will have to begin to assume more of the onus for orchestrating this revolution, and demonstrate—with the kinds of numbers profit-making companies can understand—that a movement is indeed afoot. The recording companies just won't finance it otherwise; they don't have to.

There must also be more camaraderie among jazz organizations and support groups, and a greater degree of national networking among them. They would find greater strength in increased numbers. They also need to find ways of keeping the recording companies, radio stations, other media, and the various charts alerted to changes in the marketplace and attuned to the popularity of various styles, older artists, and so on. Recording companies and jazz organizations should both develop a better rapport with the schools. College concert series bureaus meet annually to book acts for the year. Managers will have to be more creative and aggressive in pursuing these as well as other alternative venues.

Jazz is an art of processing and disseminating information in a society that, today, as Dr. Taylor has stated, is evolving from an industrial economy into an information and services economy. Jazz not only reflects this change but is feeding it as well. If there is a significant growth of interest in jazz at this time, perhaps it is partly the result of this social symbiosis. Whatever the case, jazz would do well to play the nation's campuses, where it will almost certainly find musically open minds being trained in the kinds of information processing and associative mental disciplines that make them fertile ground for the cultivation of that greater commercial audience. Today's college students are alert and looking for new signals. Quite likely, they are also already familiar with such new technology as digital sampling synthesizers, sequencers, and so on.

Another new technology, the compact disc, is serving jazz well in a way the industry may not have anticipated. By raising the standard of quality in sound reproduction, it has led some fascinated audiophiles to explore beyond rock and popular music for better writing, arranging, and musicianship. They're finding that the enhanced sound quality has more meaning when what is being reproduced has something of value to impart.

Not all new technologies have received as universal a welcome in the jazz community as the CD has. The synthesizer is viewed by some as a musical smoke screen for camouflaging meager talents. And drum machines have cut drummers out of studio work. Though the concerns of musicians and fans about the effects of the new technology upon the art and the future employment of artists are genuine, jazz, being the art of the improviser, will ultimately find ways to integrate electronics with the more traditional acoustic instrumentation. Further, the rich tradition of jazz drumming and the high level of musicianship expected by discerning jazz fans will ensure the triumph of master drummer over drum machine. The machines simply cannot match gifted musicians for musical information, texture, or subtlety. But most important, they can't improvise. The synths are here to stay, at least for a while, and they are part of the context within which the artist must improvise.

The jazz artist's ability to improvise within a given context has led to the creation of new techniques and styles, of which fusion is only one among many. Nor is it the first fusion. The infusion of East Indian and Latin elements into the music qualifies as fusion. And the blending of African rhythms with European harmonies, with the spirituals, the work songs, the blues, and the marching band music that gave birth to jazz, makes the entire tradition one based on fusion. The value of today's fusion to the jazz purist may be that it can provide an introduction or stepping-stone for some listeners from popular music to jazz. On Ramsey Lewis's album *Sun Goddess,* with the popular group Earth, Wind & Fire, the introduction of a screaming saxophone solo in a musical context its audience could easily handle may have primed some listeners for a Joe Henderson or a Pharaoh Sanders.

Inevitably, in the continuing evolution of the art, there will be an increasing variety of styles . . . and of audiences to support them. That these have been segmented into "arbitrary styles" seems to me to be partly the resultant casualties (or offspring) of two almost diametrically opposed systems of communications: those being jazz and the English language. While the former exemplifies a great deal of respect for the intelligence of the audience and its ability to interpret for itself from a broad range of possibilities, the other stems from a tradition that insists on precision of definition in everything and the use of labels to categorize things it doesn't want to think about.

A situation commonly arises in the music business today in which recording companies and artists, especially, find themselves competing against pop stars for positions on the same charts. I initiated, by way of the Jazz Committee for the Recording Industry, which I chair, two changes in the chart system at *Billboard.* As a result, there are now separate charts for contemporary and traditional jazz. This separation should prove especially advantageous to the pure jazz artist who, since he will no longer be in competition with the crossover artists for record sales, will hit higher on the charts and get more radio play. Retailers will take larger orders of the product and, withal, there will be greater opportunity for an artist to be signed by a major label.

I think there needs to be an aggressive effort on the part of jazz organizations to get to know the people at *Billboard, Cash Box, Radio and Records,* and *Down Beat*. These are people in positions of power, who are capable of determining the fate of an artist's career. As Dr. Taylor noted in his paper, jazz needs sensitive, capable professionals to work with individual artists. We need public relations people—better spokespersons for the music and the music business, and fewer angry people articulating our needs. But the artists who need these professionals most are usually those who can least afford to hire them. What is needed is people who will recognize the potential for making money, people who will make an investment in this art form. Wynton Marsalis is today that rarest of phenomena, a jazz musician who is a media star, not because he is an exceptional musician (which he is albeit one among many), but because he has professional public relations people working in his interest. He can afford them now but he couldn't always. It took someone with an expertise in marketing to recognize a potential worth investing in.

Finally, the artists themselves must begin to develop a new attitude about marketing their creations. They must begin to function as their own best press. The attitude of social aloofness that accompanied the bebop revolution and the awakening of musicians as artists is no longer a politically or professionally hip mode for making one's statement. Jazz has been recognized throughout the world as America's premier art form since the days of Charles "Buddy" Bolden, Louis Armstrong, and Sidney Bechet—and now even America is beginning to recognize it. The baby boomers are finally outgrowing rock and roll, and many are looking around and listening for music that is intellectually and emotionally more satisfying. That music can and should be jazz in all its stylistic diversity.

Recognition, Prestige, and Respect: They're Academic Questions

We have a favorite pastime in jazz—we musicians, reviewers, historians, journalists, fans. When we get together in almost any combination, the conversation will sooner or later turn to laments that jazz is not understood, does not have the respect, the prestige, the support that the music has rightfully earned and that our symphonies and our opera companies have. We have gone on to complain that established classical critics, most music educators, and others of influence not only don't know the music and don't listen to it, but are ignorant of its very nature and of the concerns and intentions of its musicians.

A great deal of what is said on such occasions may seem like self-indulgence if not downright self-pity. But that being acknowledged, it is true that jazz does lack prestige and the kind of support that goes with it, and that it could well use the kind of support that, let us say, Franz Schubert's music has in the United States.

Let's look more closely at a typical example of such support. In Washington, D.C., we have an underwritten, partly tax-supported arts complex, the Kennedy Center. New York's Lincoln Center preceded it. And large arts centers now dot our major cities while smaller ones can be found in cities with populations of perhaps 300,000 citizens.

Musically speaking, why are these centers there? Are they all there, as one might assume, because Bach, Haydn, Verdi, and the rest were great composers? And because the musical culture and tradition they represent is one that America has legitimately adopted and sees as part of its own heritage? Such a conclusion seems sound enough, but perhaps it jumps a step. The Lincoln and Kennedy and Los Angeles arts centers are not there because Handel, Brahms, and Puccini were great composers. They are there because everyone *knows* that they were great composers. Even citizens who will never be seen at our arts centers and will never buy a Beethoven recording know it. And they know it because the work on that musical tradition and its great composers has been done.

One can take Music Appreciation 101 in any third-rate college, taught by the worst dolt on the music faculty, and learn something substantial about Bach, Mozart, and Chopin, because the work of critical selection, musical analysis, biography, and music history has been done on these composers, and their scores are available. Until we do that kind of work in jazz, until we do the selection, analysis, biography, and music history, we will not have the recognition, prestige, and support we claim to want and need. Ellington may very well be *the* major figure in 20th-century American music, but unless Americans do the requisite scholarly work and critical work on him, he will surely be forgotten.

It's worth repeating: the Kennedy Center is not there because Schumann wrote some excellent music, but because everyone knows Schumann wrote some excellent music. We should remember that for over a century J. S. Bach was not considered a great composer, simply because no one had done the work on him: the work of biography, analysis, praise, and publication. When he became a great composer in everyone's thinking, his music did not change; it simply got played and heard and talked about.

One may contend, of course, that taste changed in Bach's favor. And changing taste is always a part of the risk in any received cultural activity. Bach may again fall out of favor to some extent. Tchaikovsky, for example, is nowadays falling back into favor among musical highbrows. However, with the work of criticism, publication, study, and performance of Bach's music that has gone on since the late 19th century, we may be sure that Bach will never again be thought of as he once was: historically interesting for certain techniques which his music perfected but which were old-fashioned. Bach's fashion may falter; his real reputation will not.

Let me put all of this by analogy. Shakespeare is still a living dramatist in the English-speaking world, his works still affecting millions of people directly and indirectly, and the meaning of his plays still affecting the sensibilities of western civilization—even for people who have never read him or seen him performed, and never will. But this influence is the result of a lot of linguistic study and textual analysis; a lot of editing and footnoting and publishing; a lot of biography, social and dramatic history, and literary criticism; and a lot of teaching at all levels. All that, as a source not only of the plays' survival in the classroom, but of their continuing public performance, recognition, and respect.

The story does not stop there. Almost any young dramatist who has anything valid to offer the theater automatically gains a certain prestige because of Shakespeare's high accomplishments. He works in a respected tradition, even if he is the most rebellious avant-garde figure *not* writing in that tradition.

To remove the analogy, any young jazz musician who has something to offer should gain public prestige simply by working in the tradition of Morton, Armstrong, Ellington, Parker, and Monk. Jazz musicians, and most of their followers, are not used to thinking of their music in such terms—or at any rate, they are barely beginning to. And I am not suggesting we try to turn any musicians who are not so inclined into scholars or critics. But if we want the understanding and prestige and longevity we claim to want from the world at large, all of us ought to understand the function of such scholarly and educational activities, and encourage them. Furthermore, the musicians among us might want to remember that it was a major composer, Felix Mendelssohn, who probably had the most to do with Bach's belated acceptance into the pantheon of great European masters.

Jazz musicians have traditionally had to seek out their audiences for themselves in the popular arena. They do not, like Handel and Brahms, have a large portion of that audience awarded to them by an established and prestigious cultural continuity, maintained in large part by thousands of courses in music appreciation and hundreds of courses on the symphony.

As I am implying, however, it is not only the audiences who will profit from a widespread knowledge of the music's history. There is a more personal stability and sense of purpose that such a knowledge awards the individual performers. A second viola player in a midwestern American symphony orchestra knows what musical values he represents and where he belongs in a long tradition of high accomplishment. Traditionally, most jazz musicians have not had that sense of themselves. We should be able to offer a tenor saxophonist, lucky enough to have a weekend gig, knowledge of his history and a sense of his mission, so that he may say to himself, perhaps faced with a noisy and inattentive audience, that although he may not be Coleman Hawkins or Lester Young or Sonny Rollins, he does belong with them in a music which they helped to forge so adventurously. If we can do that, I think we will have served both him and the music well.

I think I know as well as anyone that one takes great risks in submitting any artistic pursuit to the demands of scholarship, and that there are hazards in taking any aesthetic activity into the classroom. Anyone who has had Shakespeare ruined by a teacher more concerned with the state of Shakespearean scholarship than with the human insight of the plays, anyone who has had Mozart's music trivialized by a mechanical or insensitive presentation, anyone who has witnessed the history of architecture reduced to an exercise in Marxist-Leninist social theory will know how terrible the risks can be. But they are risks that have to be taken.

From such a point of view, what does jazz need? The list is enormous. Although there have been a few commendable biographies of jazz musicians, there have not been nearly enough. I will cite only Coleman Hawkins and Art Tatum as two major figures with no biographies; the knowledgeable mind can easily prepare a list of its own.

Scores? The works of Duke Ellington, whether they can be gleaned from surviving written materials or must be notated from recordings, should be published in complete authoritative editions. But Ellington's works would merely be a beginning. Every American music library should have its Don Redman and Fletcher Henderson collections; its Sy Oliver, Edgar Sampson, and Jimmy Mundy volumes; its Gil Evans—but the list (again) is a long one.

I need only mention, surely, that the critical history of the music undertaken by Gunther Schuller still stands virtually alone. And what if we had a detailed study of Ellington's harmonic language, and of Billy Strayhorn's? At a practical level, we might save future American composers and orchestrators a decade of work out of their careers. At an artistic level, well, think of the possibilities.

Furthermore, we are still plagued with basic classroom texts on jazz history that are inadequate. One of them is by now fairly notorious for constant inaccuracies in its musical examples and analyses, and for its almost page-by-page mistakes of fact. Almost all of them give away the author's age in that the writer clearly gives greater emphasis and praise to the period of his own adolescent awakenings to the music.

Walter Allen's monumental bio-discographies of King Oliver and Fletcher Henderson should not only be a source of pride for us all but should be the models for dozens of such studies, and I assume I do not need to name artists' names here to affirm the need. Meanwhile, all of us would do well to know about and welcome discographical work on Eric Dolphy; and we should know Lewis Porter's study of

Lester Young, Thomas Owens's microfilmed but still unpublished study of Charlie Parker's style, Jerry Valburn's compilation of Ellington's nonstudio recordings, Arnold Laubich's Art Tatum discography. Even those of us who may never use or read such studies should know of such activities because their very existence benefits us all, musicians and audiences, as well as teachers, journalists, and historians. The seriousness of such work is a major source of the attention and prestige we need.

Actually, jazz musicians in their own ways have taken similar approaches to history and tradition. A prominent bass player, while recently expressing puzzlement and even condescension toward the scholarly writing and analysis that is now beginning in jazz, admitted in almost the same breath that he had developed his own craft by notating Jimmy Blanton's bass parts and learning them. And Ray Brown's. And by seeing how he could meet the great challenge of Mingus, by sheading with Charlie's records. He was even grateful, he added, to a record-collector friend who showed him how Walter Page's strong lead in the Basie rhythm section rewrote the history of the instrument ("wrong" notes or not), and how Johnny Lindsey's strong 1920s sound was not the simple bass "slapping" of the period.

I am not proposing the sort of musicological research, music history, and biography, evaluation, and analysis that has as its real purpose only the production of still more musicology. I have in mind some very practical matters. For one, it is simply wrong—morally and artistically wrong, if you will—that concert after concert by our student jazz orchestras goes by without a single jazz classic on the program. At best, we may get a *Moonlight Serenade* in a chorus-and-a-half for the old folks, or we get someone's arrangement of a familiar Ellington tune (reorchestrating Ellington makes about as much sense as reorchestrating Ravel or Stravinsky, and for the very same reason).

I think that any student trained in jazz performance should know what Ferd Morton, Don Redman, Fletcher Henderson, (above all) Duke Ellington, Thelonious Monk, and the other major composer/orchestrators have contributed to the music. He should know intimately what Louis Armstrong, Lester Young, and Charlie Parker stood for as improvisers (that is, as spontaneous linear composers) and he should know these things not only by hearing them on recordings but by performing them. And performing them, not only as an honorable musical past from which he can learn, but as a body of living musical art that is regularly brought before audiences. A music that has no past worthy of serious attention probably has little present, and may have no future at all. And the past should be the concern of all of us ultimately for the sake of the music's audiences, present and future.

We might even envision a time when a student clarinetist, graduating from a jazz performance program, will be required to improvise respectably well in the styles of Sidney Bechet, Jimmie Noone, Omer Simeon, Benny Goodman, and Barney Bigard. Or a tenor saxophonist give a chorus or two after Coleman Hawkins, Lester Young, Dexter Gordon, Sonny Rollins, John Coltrane, ending (surely) with choruses in an approach of his own.

In short, we all need to show that we are absolutely serious about this music as a contribution to world culture. And that means that we must treat it in the same way that we have always treated a past that we want preserved and respected for the sake of the present and the future.

Appendix A:
Notes on the Contributors

Amiri Baraka (LeRoi Jones) is an author, playwright, social critic/observer of the human scene, director, editor, and faculty member. A prolific writer, he has produced more than twenty-six plays, twelve books of poetry, ten fiction and nonfiction books, and four anthologies.

He was commissioned by the Paris Opéra to write *Jazz Opera* in collaboration with the Swiss composer George Gruntz. His latest book, *The Music: Reflections on Blues and Jazz,* with Amina Baraka, was published by William Morrow.

Baraka is currently teaching as a visiting professor at Rutgers University (while on leave as director of African Studies at the State University of New York at Stony Brook). He was founder, organizer, and director of the Black Arts Repertory Theatre-School (BARTS), which influenced and inspired black theaters throughout the country. He also founded Spirit House, a black repertory theater and cultural center. Currently he is co-coordinator with Amina Baraka of Kimako's Blues People, an arts performance space in Newark.

A recipient of Guggenheim and Whitney fellowships, he has won awards from the National Endowment for the Arts for poetry, the Rockefeller Foundation for drama, and the prestigious Obie Award for Best American Play. He has received an honorary Doctor of Humane Letters from Malcolm X College in Chicago.

George Butler is vice president/executive producer of CBS Records, a lecturer, a concert producer, and a jazz and classical clinician. His areas of specialization are classical, jazz/progressive, and contemporary music.

Formerly associated with United Artists Records, he later held positions as director, vice president, and general manager of Blue Note Records, the jazz label of United Artists.

As a producer, Butler has received over 50 gold records. He has been producer or executive producer for the following Grammy winners: Duke Ellington, Miles Davis, Wynton Marsalis (six Grammys, making history by winning in two distinctly different categories—jazz and classical), Herbie Hancock, Maynard Ferguson, and Weather Report.

He has produced concerts at the Hollywood Bowl and the Dorothy Chandler Pavilion in Los Angeles, Carnegie Hall in New York, the Montreux Jazz Festival in Montreux, Switzerland, and the San Francisco Opera House.

He has lectured at the universities of Massachusetts, Pittsburgh, Miami, and Minnesota; New York University; Berklee College of Music; and Manhattan School of Music. He has conducted jazz and classical workshops and clinics at Yale, Temple, Rutgers, and Southern universities, as well as in Germany, France, the Netherlands, and Mexico.

He received the Bachelor of Music degree from Howard University, Master of Music degrees from Yale and Columbia universities, and the Ph.D. degree from Columbia.

John Conyers, Jr., Congressman, First District, Michigan, was reelected in 1988 to his thirteenth term in the U.S. House of Representatives, winning 92 percent of the vote. He is senior member of the Judiciary Committee, is chairman of the Government Operations Committee, and also serves on the Small Business Committee.

During his twenty-five years on Capitol Hill, economic opportunities and social justice have become focal points of Congressman Conyers's efforts. He has introduced legislation for economic and community development, minority business set-asides, social security, civil and constitutional rights, education, and criminal justice. In addition, he has cosponsored over 300 pieces of legislation.

Congressman Conyers authored and spearheaded the drive for passage of the Martin Luther King holiday bill; is one of the architects of the Congressional Black Caucus's annual alternative budget; offered the first nuclear freeze amendment that would have deleted funds for the further testing, production, and deployment of new nuclear warheads and missiles while freezing existing stockpiles; and introduced an amendment prohibiting the export of nuclear-related materials, technology, equipment, information, and personnel to South Africa, which became a part of the House-approved Anti-Apartheid Act.

In the fall of 1987, the Congress passed House Concurrent Resolution 57, a measure introduced by Congressman Conyers designating jazz as an "American National Treasure." In February 1989, he introduced House Joint Resolution 662, legislation designating May 25 as "National Tap Dance Day." This measure passed the House on May 25, 1989. Since 1985, Congressman Conyers has hosted the annual Congressional Black Caucus Foundation Weekend Jazz and Arts Issues Forums.

Congressman Conyers received his bachelor's and Doctor of Law degrees from Wayne State University in Detroit.

Stanley Crouch writes about jazz, politics, ethnic issues, theater, and literature for publications such as the *Village Voice* and *The New*

Republic. In 1990, three books of his will be published: *Notes of a Hanging Judge*, essays; *In the Language of Papa Dip and Duke*, jazz writing; and *First Snow in Koko*, a novel. For the past seven years, he has been researching an extensive biography of Charlie Parker. He is also working with Wynton Marsalis on a musical about Louis Armstrong.

He taught the history of jazz, American and Afro-American literature, theater, and literary analysis at the Claremont Colleges in southern California for seven years. He was a staff writer for the *Village Voice* from 1980 to 1988 and is currently artistic consultant for the Classical Jazz concert series at Lincoln Center.

Gary Giddins has published over 500 essays on music, books, and films. His jazz column, "Weather Bird," has appeared since 1973 in the *Village Voice*, where he is a staff writer. It won the ASCAP–Deems Taylor Award for general excellence in music criticism in 1976, 1977, and 1984. He has also won a Merit Award from the Art Directors Club for the jazz supplements he edits annually in the *Village Voice* (1985); a Guggenheim Fellowship (1986); the American Book Award and the ASCAP–Deems Taylor Award for his book *Celebrating Bird: The Triumph of Charlie Parker* (1987); the American Video Conference Award for his documentary film *Celebrating Bird* (1988); and an honorary degree in fine arts from Grinnell College (1988).

Giddins has taught jazz history at the University of Pennsylvania, Rutgers University, and New York University's School of Continuing Education. He is currently on the faculty of the Writing Program at Columbia University. He has produced concerts, recordings, and a radio series. In 1985 he founded the American Jazz Orchestra, an 18-piece repertory ensemble with John Lewis as music director and chief conductor. The orchestra concluded its third season in April 1989, and has recorded two albums, *Central City Sketches* with Benny Carter and *Ellington Masterpieces* conducted by Lewis.

Giddins's books include *Riding on a Blue Note* (Oxford, 1981), *Rhythm-a-ning* (Oxford, 1985), *Celebrating Bird: The Triumph of Charlie Parker* (Beech Tree, 1986), and *Satchmo* (Doubleday, 1989). He adapted the last two as documentary films, which were broadcast by PBS stations in July 1989.

Harold Horowitz, director of research for the National Endowment for the Arts from 1975 to his retirement in 1988, managed an active research agenda of studies related to artists, arts organizations, and audiences throughout the United States. Under his direction, the Endowment put into place a continuing Survey of Public Participation in the Arts. The paper published in this book, "The American Jazz Audience," reports the findings related to jazz from the survey conducted in 1982.

Horowitz is an architect with a B.A. degree in architecture from the Institute of Design of the Illinois Institute of Technology in Chicago and a master's degree in architecture from the Massachusetts Institute of Technology in Cambridge. He is a registered architect in New Jersey and Maryland and a member emeritus of the American Institute of Architects.

Horowitz has balanced his career between the arts and science, keeping him on the cutting edge of the creation and application of new technology at the National Academy of Sciences' National Research Council, 1955–63; the National Science Foundation, 1963–75; and the National Endowment for the Arts, 1975–88. His enthusiasm for jazz stems from his youth in Chicago, where he lived a short walk from several jazz clubs on Howard Street.

Jimmy Lyons is founder of the oldest continuous jazz festival in the world, the Monterey Jazz Festival, which has been a showcase for performers for almost three decades. In recent years, the festival's educational aspects have assumed increased importance through the training of high school students in jazz.

Lyons was the advance publicist for the Woody Herman Band, and has worked with Stan Kenton and other jazz artists. He has held the positions of executive secretary and chair of the California Arts Council, and has been actively involved in jazz presentations sponsored by the U.S. Department of State.

He has written, produced, and broadcast jazz radio programs in Carmel, San Diego, and San Francisco, and has written and produced "Jubilee," a jazz programming series for the American Armed Forces. He studied at the University of California and Columbia University.

Dan Morgenstern, director of the Institute of Jazz Studies (IJS) at Rutgers University since 1976, is a jazz historian, author, and editor professionally active in the jazz field since 1958. He is co-editor of the *Annual Review of Jazz Studies*, published by IJS and Transaction Books, and the *Studies in Jazz* series, published by IJS and Scarecrow Press.

A frequent contributor to the jazz and generalist press, Morgenstern is the author of *Jazz People* (Harry N. Abrams, 1976), served as the editor of *Down Beat* from 1967 to 1973, and was that magazine's New York editor from 1964 to 1966. He was also editor of the periodicals *Jazz* and *Metronome*, jazz critic for the *New York Post* and the *Chicago Sun-Times*, and U.S. correspondent for Japan's *Swing Journal* and Great Britain's *Jazz Journal*. He has contributed to numerous anthologies and reference works, including the *Encyclopedia Britannica Book of the Year*, the *American Grove*, the *New Grove Dictionary of Jazz*, and the *Musician's Guide*.

Morgenstern has taught jazz history at the Peabody Institute in Baltimore, at New York University, and at Brooklyn College, where he was also a visiting professor at the Institute for Studies in American Music. He has also served on the faculty of the institutes in jazz criticism jointly sponsored by the Smithsonian Institution and the Music Critics Association.

Morgenstern has been active in concert production, broadcasting, and record reissue production. A prolific annotator of record albums, he has won Grammy Awards for Best Album Notes in 1973, 1974, 1976, and 1981. He received the ASCAP–Deems Taylor Award for *Jazz People*.

Cofounder and director of the Jazz Institute of Chicago, Morgenstern served on the board of directors of the New York Jazz Museum, and is a director of the Mary Lou Williams Foundation. He is a vice president, trustee, and New York chapter governor of the

National Academy of Recording Arts and Sciences, and has served as a panel cochair, panelist, and consultant to the Jazz Program of the National Endowment for the Arts.

Gunther Schuller, composer, conductor, educator, author, publisher, and administrator, currently holds the positions of founder and music director of the Boston Composers Orchestra and director of the Festival at Sandpoint (Idaho). He has previously been artistic director of the Berkshire Music Center, president of the New England Conservatory of Music, and a faculty member at the Manhattan School of Music and Yale University.

A prolific composer who has been active in jazz performance, Schuller has sought to combine jazz elements with the classical music tradition. He has written in most media, including opera, ballet, orchestral music, concerted works, chamber music, and vocal music. He has been commissioned by the Fromm, Ford, and Koussevitzky foundations, the New York Philharmonic, and the Donaueschingen Contemporary Music Festival, to name a few.

He travels to Europe annually as a guest conductor for orchestras such as the Berlin Philharmonic, BBC Symphony, French Radio Orchestra, Helsinki Philharmonic, and Halle Concert Society, in addition to his frequent guest appearances in the United States. He has written books on horn technique and on jazz.

A member of the American Academy of Arts and Letters since 1980, Schuller has received honorary degrees from Northwestern University, the University of Illinois, Colby College, Williams College, New England Conservatory, and Rutgers University. He has received two Guggenheim Fellowships, the Darius Milhaud Award, the Alic M. Ditson Conducting Award, and the Rodgers and Hammerstein Award. He is a member of the National Institute of Arts and Letters and has served on the National Council on the Arts.

Billy Taylor, pianist, composer, educator, and consultant, has been credited with bringing jazz to the forums of national radio and television. An articulate spokesperson for jazz, he won Peabody

Awards for his 13-part National Public Radio series "Taylor-Made Piano" and "Jazz Alive," and an Emmy Award for a segment of the CBS-TV "Sunday Morning" program, where he was the on-the-air correspondent. The first black artist to host a daily show on a major New York radio station, he also hosted special music programs and interviews on the National Educational Network, was producer and host of "The Billy Taylor Show," and contributing editor and on-camera performer of the weekly shows "Black Journal" on PBS and "Sunday" on NBC in New York. He was music director for the award-winning "David Frost Show," "Black Journal Tonight," "The Subject Is Jazz," and "That Was The Week That Was." In addition, he was music director and arranger for the play "Your Arms Too Short to Box with God." He consults with and advises radio and television stations, music schools, and civic and cultural groups.

As a pianist, Billy Taylor runs the gamut from solo recitals to performances with symphony orchestras. He has led his own trio for thirty years. He has been featured soloist with all-star groups that have included Charlie Parker, Dizzy Gillespie, Miles Davis, and Art Blakey. He won the first International Critics Award from *Down Beat* for best pianist. He has recorded more than two dozen albums of his own, and now has his own label, Taylor-Made Jazz.

He has written more than 300 songs and several movie scores. His commissioned works have been performed by more than fifty orchestras, including the Atlanta Symphony, the Indianapolis Symphony, and the Utah Symphony.

Taylor conducts clinics and workshops on improvisation, piano styles, harmony, theory, and composition at major universities and colleges. His latest book, *Jazz Piano: A Jazz History*, is offered as a credit course to college music majors in conjunction with cassettes. He has written twelve other books on jazz and jazz piano playing. He is also founder and president of Jazzmobile Inc. in New York City.

Taylor earned a combined master's degree and doctorate in education from the University of Massachusetts and has since been awarded with six honorary doctorates from various colleges and universities.

Martin Williams is an acquisitions editor for the Smithsonian Institution Press and a critic, researcher, and lecturer. He selected and annotated the recorded anthology *The Smithsonian Collection of Classic Jazz*. He previously served as director of the Jazz and American Culture Program at the Smithsonian Institution.

His career as a writer on the American arts, particularly jazz, spans over thirty years. In addition to reviews and scholarly research published in this country and abroad, he has published six books on jazz, including the biographical critical study *Jazz Masters of New Orleans* and the well-received critical work *The Jazz Tradition*. He is the author of *Jazz in Its Time, Jazz Heritage,* and *Where's the Melody?* and was general editor of the Macmillan "Jazz Masters" series. He cofounded and coedited *The Jazz Review*.

He has taught courses in jazz history at the New School, Rutgers University, the Peabody Institute, the Smithsonian Institution, Brooklyn College of the City University of New York, the University of Maryland, and Virginia Commonwealth University. He has lectured widely on jazz, film, and children's literature at Princeton, Harvard, Sarah Lawrence, Bennington, Bard, Emory, Oberlin, and many other institutions. Pursuing other aspects of American culture, he has written on film, the musical stage, theater, children's literature, the comic strip, and television.

He received a Grammy Award for album notes to *The Smithsonian Collection of Big Band Jazz* (written with Gunther Schuller), and twice received the ASCAP–Deems Taylor Award for excellence in music criticism. He was a Guggenheim Fellow, and a Senior Research Fellow at the Institute for Studies in American Music at Brooklyn College of the City University of New York.

He is a graduate of the University of Virginia and the University of Pennsylvania.

Olly Wilson is professor of music and director of the Electronic Music Program at the University of California–Berkeley. In the forefront of electronic music since 1967, he has lectured on electronic and contemporary music topics at numerous colleges, universities, and conservatories, and at music, anthropological, and writers' conferences in Europe, Africa, and America.

A prolific composer, Wilson has received commissions from the Boston Symphony Orchestra, the Fromm Foundation, Pitzer College, the Oakland Symphony Orchestra, the San Francisco Chamber Music Society, the San Francisco Contemporary Music Ensemble, and the American Composers Orchestra, to name a few. His works have been performed at the Third International Electronic Avant-Garde 85 Festival, Chicago; the American Academy in Rome; on concert tours in Europe, Australia, and New Zealand; and at the Kennedy Center, the Composers-International Society for Contemporary Music at Carnegie Hall, and the Cantiere Internazionale d'Arte Festival in Montepulciano, Italy.

At the first international competition for electronic music, Wilson received the Dartmouth Arts Council Prize in 1968 for his work *Cetus*. He has received two Guggenheim Fellowships, the Regents Faculty Fellowship, and two Humanities Research Fellowships. He has received annual awards (from 1971 to the present) from the American Society for Composers, Arrangers and Performers, the Award of Distinction from the National Association of Negro Musicians, and the Award for Achievement in Music Composition from the American Academy of Arts and Letters and the National Institute of Arts and Letters.

He holds degrees from Washington University in St. Louis, the University of Illinois, and the University of Iowa.

Appendix B:
Conference Participants

Muhal Richard Abrams
Association for the Advancement of
Creative Musicians

David N. Baker
National Jazz Service Organization

Edward Birdwell
National Endowment for the Arts

William B. Boyd
The Johnson Foundation

George Butler
CBS Records

Warrick Carter
Berklee College of Music

Richie Cole
Saxophonist

J. Richard Dunscomb
National Association of Jazz
Educators

Vince Giordano
Multi-Instrumentalist

Eugene Grissom
American Federation of Jazz
Societies

D. Antoinette Handy
National Endowment for the Arts

Frank Hodsoll
National Endowment for the Arts

James Jordan
National Jazz Service Organization

Burt Korall
Broadcast Music Incorporated (BMI)

Eunice Lockhart-Moss
National Jazz Service Organization

Bruce McDonald
Berklee College of Music

Cobi Narita
Universal Jazz Coalition

Lee Nordness
The Keland Endowment Fund

Earl Palmer
National Academy of Recording Arts
and Sciences
Musicians Union Local 47

Susan Poulsen-Krogh
The Johnson Foundation

Harvey G. Phillips
Indiana University School of Music

Larry Ridley
Bassist

James T. Rohner
The Instrumentalist

Henrietta Sanford
National Jazz Service Organization

Vivian Scott
American Society of Composers,
Authors, and Publishers

Victoria Sharpley
National Jazz Service Organization

Ann Sneed
International Art of Jazz

Ken Sunshine
American Society of Composers,
Authors, and Publishers

William E. Terry
National Jazz Service Organization

Frederick C. Tillis
University of Massachusetts
at Amherst

Herb Wong
Blackhawk Records

Appendix C:
Conference Planning Committee

David N. Baker, Chair
National Jazz Service Organization

Warrick Carter
Berklee College of Music

Eunice Lockhart-Moss
National Jazz Service Organization

Bruce McDonald
Berklee College of Music

Susan Poulsen-Krogh
The Johnson Foundation

Frederick C. Tillis
University of Massachusetts
at Amherst

For further information concerning the New Perspectives on Jazz conference and project, contact the National Jazz Service Organization, Gallery Row, 409 Seventh Street NW, Washington, D.C. 20004-0061; (202) 347- 2604.